Travel phrasebooks collection
«Everything Will Be Okay!»

T&P Books Publishing

CW00548521

PHRAS

- AFRIKAANS -

By Andrey Taranov

THE MOST IMPORTANT PHRASES

This phrasebook contains the most important phrases and questions for basic communication
Everything you need to survive overseas

T&p BOOKS

Phrasebook + 3000-word dictionary

English-Afrikaans phrasebook & topical vocabulary

By Andrey Taranov

The collection of "Everything Will Be Okay" travel phrasebooks published by T&P Books is designed for people traveling abroad for tourism and business. The phrasebooks contain what matters most - the essentials for basic communication. This is an indispensable set of phrases to "survive" while abroad.

This book also includes a small topical vocabulary that contains roughly 3,000 of the most frequently used words. Another section of the phrasebook provides a gastronomical dictionary that may help you order food at a restaurant or buy groceries at the store.

T&P Books Publishing
www.tpbooks.com

ISBN: 978-1-78716-573-1

This book is also available in E-book formats.
Please visit www.tpbooks.com or the major online bookstores.

FOREWORD

The collection of "Everything Will Be Okay" travel phrasebooks published by T&P Books is designed for people traveling abroad for tourism and business. The phrasebooks contain what matters most - the essentials for basic communication. This is an indispensable set of phrases to "survive" while abroad.

This phrasebook will help you in most cases where you need to ask something, get directions, find out how much something costs, etc. It can also resolve difficult communication situations where gestures just won't help.

This book contains a lot of phrases that have been grouped according to the most relevant topics. The edition also includes a small vocabulary that contains roughly 3,000 of the most frequently used words. Another section of the phrasebook provides a gastronomical dictionary that may help you order food at a restaurant or buy groceries at the store.

Take "Everything Will Be Okay" phrasebook with you on the road and you'll have an irreplaceable traveling companion who will help you find your way out of any situation and teach you to not fear speaking with foreigners.

TABLE OF CONTENTS

T&P Books Publishing

PRONUNCIATION

T&P phonetic alphabet	Afrikaans example	English example
[a]	land	shorter than in ask
[ā]	straat	calf, palm
[æ]	hout	chess, man
[o], [ɔ]	Australië	drop, baught
[e]	metaal	elm, medal
[ɛ]	aanlê	man, bad
[ə]	filter	driver, teacher
[ɪ]	uur	big, America
[i]	billik	shorter than in feet
[ï]	naïef	tree, big
[o]	koppie	pod, John
[ø]	akteur	eternal, church
[œ]	fluit	German Hölle
[u]	hulle	book
[ʊ]	hout	good, booklet
[b]	bakker	baby, book
[d]	donder	day, doctor
[f]	navraag	face, food
[g]	burger	game, gold
[h]	driehoek	home, have
[j]	byvoeg	yes, New York
[k]	kamera	clock, kiss
[l]	loon	lace, people
[m]	môre	magic, milk
[n]	neef	sang, thing
[p]	pyp	pencil, private
[r]	rigting	rice, radio
[s]	oplos	city, boss
[t]	lood, tenk	tourist, trip
[v]	bewaar	very, river
[w]	oorwinnaar	vase, winter
[z]	zoem	zebra, please
[dʒ]	enjin	joke, general
[ʃ]	artisjok	machine, shark
[ŋ]	kans	English, ring

T&P phonetic alphabet	Afrikaans example	English example
[ʧ]	tjek	church, French
[ʒ]	beige	forge, pleasure
[x]	agent	as in Scots 'loch'

LIST OF ABBREVIATIONS

English abbreviations

ab.	-	about
adj	-	adjective
adv	-	adverb
anim.	-	animate
as adj	-	attributive noun used as adjective
e.g.	-	for example
etc.	-	et cetera
fam.	-	familiar
fem.	-	feminine
form.	-	formal
inanim.	-	inanimate
masc.	-	masculine
math	-	mathematics
mil.	-	military
n	-	noun
pl	-	plural
pron.	-	pronoun
sb	-	somebody
sing.	-	singular
sth	-	something
v aux	-	auxiliary verb
vi	-	intransitive verb
vi, vt	-	intransitive, transitive verb
vt	-	transitive verb

AFRIKAANS PHRASEBOOK

This section contains important phrases that may come in handy in various real-life situations.
The phrasebook will help you ask for directions, clarify a price, buy tickets, and order food at a restaurant

T&P Books Publishing

PHRASEBOOK
CONTENTS

T&P Books Publishing

The bare minimum

Excuse me, ...	**Verskoon my, ...** [ferskoən maj, ...]
Hello.	**Hallo.** [hallo.]
Thank you.	**Baie dankie.** [baje danki.]
Good bye.	**Totsiens.** [totsiŋs.]
Yes.	**Ja.** [ja.]
No.	**Nee.** [neə.]
I don't know.	**Ek weet nie.** [ɛk veət ni.]
Where? | Where to? | When?	**Waar? | Waarheen? | Wanneer?** [vār? | vārheən? | vanneər?]
I need ...	**Ek het ... nodig** [ɛk het ... nodəχ]
I want ...	**Ek wil ...** [ɛk vil ...]
Do you have ...?	**Het u ...?** [het u ...?]
Is there a ... here?	**Is hier 'n ...?** [is hir ə ...?]
May I ...?	**Mag ek ...?** [maχ ek ...?]
..., please (polite request)	**... asseblief** [... asseblif]
I'm looking for ...	**Ek soek ...** [ɛk suk ...]
restroom	**toilet** [tojlet]
ATM	**OTM** [o·te·em]
pharmacy (drugstore)	**apteek** [apteək]
hospital	**hospitaal** [hospitāl]
police station	**polisiekantoor** [polisi·kantoər]
subway	**moltrein** [moltræjn]

taxi	**taxi** [taksi]
train station	**stasie** [stasi]

My name is …	**My naam is …** [maj nām is …]
What's your name?	**Wat is u naam?** [vat is u nām?]
Could you please help me?	**Kan u my help, asseblief?** [kan u maj hɛlp, asseblif?]
I've got a problem.	**Ek het 'n probleem.** [ɛk het ə probleəm.]
I don't feel well.	**Ek voel nie lekker nie.** [ɛk ful ni lɛkkər ni.]
Call an ambulance!	**Bel 'n ambulans!** [bel ə ambulaŋs!]
May I make a call?	**Kan ek 'n oproep maak?** [kan ɛk ə oprup māk?]

I'm sorry.	**Jammer.** [jammər.]
You're welcome.	**Plesier.** [plesir.]

I, me	**Ek, my** [ek, maj]
you (inform.)	**jy** [jaj]
he	**hy** [haj]
she	**sy** [saj]
they (masc.)	**hulle** [hullə]
they (fem.)	**hulle** [hullə]
we	**ons** [ɔŋs]
you (pl)	**julle** [jullə]
you (sg, form.)	**u** [u]

ENTRANCE	**INGANG** [inχaŋ]
EXIT	**UITGANG** [œitχaŋ]
OUT OF ORDER	**BUITE WERKING** [bœitə verkiŋ]
CLOSED	**GESLUIT** [χeslœit]

OPEN	**OOP**
	[oəp]
FOR WOMEN	**DAMES**
	[dames]
FOR MEN	**MANS**
	[maŋs]

Questions

Where?	**Waar?** [vār?]
Where to?	**Waarheen?** [vārheən?]
Where from?	**Van waar?** [fan vār?]
Why?	**Waar?** [vār?]
For what reason?	**Waarom?** [vārom?]
When?	**Wanneer?** [vanneər?]
How long?	**Hoe lank?** [hu lank?]
At what time?	**Hoe laat?** [hu lāt?]
How much?	**Hoeveel?** [hufeəl?]
Do you have ...?	**Het u ...?** [het u ...?]
Where is ...?	**Waar is ...?** [vār is ...?]
What time is it?	**Hoe laat is dit?** [hu lāt is dit?]
May I make a call?	**Kan ek 'n oproep maak?** [kan ɛk ə oprup māk?]
Who's there?	**Wie is daar?** [vi is dār?]
Can I smoke here?	**Mag ek hier rook?** [maχ ek hir roək?]
May I ...?	**Mag ek ...?** [maχ ek ...?]

Needs

I'd like …	**Ek sou graag …** [ɛk sæʊ χrāχ …]
I don't want …	**Ek wil nie …** [ɛk vil ni …]
I'm thirsty.	**Ek is dors.** [ɛk is dors.]
I want to sleep.	**Ek wil slaap.** [ɛk vil slāp.]
I want …	**Ek wil …** [ɛk vil …]
to wash up	**was** [vas]
to brush my teeth	**my tande borsel** [maj tandə borsəl]
to rest a while	**bietjie rus** [biki rus]
to change my clothes	**ander klere aantrek** [andər klerə āntrek]
to go back to the hotel	**teruggaan hotel toe** [teruχχān hotəl tu]
to buy …	**… koop** [… koəp]
to go to …	**gaan na …** [χān na …]
to visit …	**besoek …** [besuk …]
to meet with …	**ontmoet …** [ontmut …]
to make a call	**bel** [bəl]
I'm tired.	**Ek is moeg.** [ɛk is muχ.]
We are tired.	**Ons is moeg.** [ɔŋs is muχ.]
I'm cold.	**Ek kry koud.** [ɛk kraj kæʊt.]
I'm hot.	**Ek kry warm.** [ɛk kraj varm.]
I'm OK.	**Ek is OK.** [ɛk is okej.]

I need to make a call.

Ek moet 'n oproep maak.
[ɛk mut ə oprup mãk.]

I need to go to the restroom.

Ek moet toilet toe gaan.
[ɛk mut toilet tu χãn.]

I have to go.

Ek moet loop.
[ɛk mut loəp.]

I have to go now.

Ek moet nou loop.
[ɛk mut næʊ loəp.]

Asking for directions

Excuse me, ...	**Verskoon tog, ...** [ferskoən toχ, ...]
Where is ...?	**Waar is ...?** [vār is ...?]
Which way is ...?	**In watter rigting is ...?** [in vattər riχtiŋ is ...?]
Could you help me, please?	**Kan u my help, asseblief?** [kan u maj hɛlp, asseblif?]
I'm looking for ...	**Ek soek ...** [ɛk suk ...]
I'm looking for the exit.	**Waar is die uitgang?** [vār is di œitχaŋ?]
I'm going to ...	**Ek gaan na ...** [ɛk χān na ...]
Am I going the right way to ...?	**Is dit die regte pad na ...?** [is dit di reχtə pat na ...?]
Is it far?	**Is dit ver?** [is dit fer?]
Can I get there on foot?	**Kan ek te voet soontoe gaan?** [kan ɛk tə fut soentu χān?]
Can you show me on the map?	**Kan u dit op die kaart aanwys?** [kan u dit op di kārt ānwajs?]
Show me where we are right now.	**Kan u my aanwys waar ons nou is?** [kan u maj ānwajs vār ɔŋs næʋ is?]
Here	**Hier** [hir]
There	**Daar** [dār]
This way	**Hiernatoe** [hirnatu]
Turn right.	**Draai regs.** [drāj reχs.]
Turn left.	**Draai links.** [drāj links.]
first (second, third) turn	**eerste (tweede, derde) draai** [eərstə (tweədə, derdə) drāi]

to the right   **na regs**
                [na reχs]

to the left   **na links**
                [na links]

Go straight ahead.   **Gaan reguit vorentoe.**
                      [χān reχœit forentu.]

Signs

WELCOME!	**WELKOM!** [vɛlkom!]
ENTRANCE	**INGANG** [inχaŋ]
EXIT	**UITGANG** [œitχaŋ]
PUSH	**STOOT** [stoət]
PULL	**TREK** [trek]
OPEN	**OOP** [oəp]
CLOSED	**GESLUIT** [χeslœit]
FOR WOMEN	**DAMES** [dames]
FOR MEN	**MANS (M)** [maŋs]
GENTLEMEN, GENTS (m)	**MANS (M)** [maŋs]
WOMEN (f)	**DAMES (V)** [dames]
DISCOUNTS	**AFSLAG** [afslaχ]
SALE	**UITVERKOPING** [œitferkopiŋ]
FREE	**GRATIS** [χratis]
NEW!	**NUUT!** [nɪt!]
ATTENTION!	**PAS OP!** [pas op!]
NO VACANCIES	**KAMERS BESET** [kamers beset]
RESERVED	**BESPREEK** [bespreək]
ADMINISTRATION	**ADMINISTRASIE** [administrasi]
STAFF ONLY	**SLEGS PERSONEEL** [sleχs personeəl]

BEWARE OF THE DOG!	**PAS OP VIR DIE HOND** [pas op fir di hont]
NO SMOKING!	**ROOK VERBODE!** [roək ferbodə!]
DO NOT TOUCH!	**NIE AANRAAK NIE!** [ni ānrāk ni!]
DANGEROUS	**GEVAARLIK** [χefārlik]
DANGER	**GEVAAR** [χefār]
HIGH VOLTAGE	**HOOGSPANNING** [hoəχ·spanniŋ]
NO SWIMMING!	**SWEM VERBODE!** [swem ferbodə!]
OUT OF ORDER	**BUITE GEBRUIK** [bœitə χebrœik]
FLAMMABLE	**BRANDBAAR** [brantbār]
FORBIDDEN	**VERBODE** [ferbodə]
NO TRESPASSING!	**TOEGANG VERBODE!** [tuχaŋ ferbodə!]
WET PAINT	**NAT VERF** [nat ferf]
CLOSED FOR RENOVATIONS	**GESLUIT VIR HERSTELWERK** [χeslœit fir herstəl·werk]
WORKS AHEAD	**PADWERKE** [padwerkə]
DETOUR	**OMPAD** [ompat]

Transportation. General phrases

plane	**vliegtuig** [fliχtœiχ]
train	**trein** [træjn]
bus	**bus** [bus]
ferry	**veerboot** [feǝr·boǝt]
taxi	**taxi** [taksi]
car	**motor** [motor]
schedule	**diensrooster** [diŋs·roǝstǝr]
Where can I see the schedule?	**Waar is die diensrooster?** [vãr is di diŋs·roǝster?]
workdays (weekdays)	**werksdae** [verksdaǝ]
weekends	**naweke** [navekǝ]
holidays	**vakansies** [fakaŋsis]
DEPARTURE	**VERTREK** [fertrek]
ARRIVAL	**AANKOMS** [ãnkoms]
DELAYED	**VERTRAAG** [fertrãχ]
CANCELLED	**GEKANSELLEER** [χekaŋsɛlleǝr]
next (train, etc.)	**volgende** [folχendǝ]
first	**eerste** [eǝrstǝ]
last	**laaste** [lãstǝ]
When is the next ...?	**Wanneer vertrek die volgende ...?** [vanneǝr fertrek di folχendǝ ...?]
When is the first ...?	**Wanneer vertrek die eerste ...?** [vanneǝr fertrek di eǝrstǝ ...?]

When is the last ...?

Wanneer vertrek die laaste ...?
[vanneǝr fertrek di lāstǝ ...?]

transfer (change of trains, etc.)

aansluiting
[āŋslœitiŋ]

to make a transfer

oorstap
[oǝrstap]

Do I need to make a transfer?

Moet ek oorstap?
[mut ek oǝrstap?]

Buying tickets

Where can I buy tickets?	**Waar kan ek kaartjies koop?** [vār kan ɛk kārkis koəp?]
ticket	**kaartjie** [kārki]
to buy a ticket	**'n kaartjie koop** [ə kārki koəp]
ticket price	**kaartjie se prys** [kārki sə prajs]

Where to?	**Waarheen?** [vārheən?]
To what station?	**Na watter stasie?** [na vattər stasi?]
I need ...	**Ek het ... nodig** [ɛk het ... nodəχ]
one ticket	**'n kaartjie** [ə kārki]
two tickets	**twee kaartjies** [tweə kārkis]
three tickets	**drie kaartjies** [dri kārkis]

one-way	**enkel** [ɛnkəl]
round-trip	**retoer** [retur]
first class	**eerste klas** [eərstə klas]
second class	**tweede klas** [tweədə klas]

today	**vandag** [fandaχ]
tomorrow	**môre** [mɔrə]
the day after tomorrow	**oormôre** [oərmɔrə]
in the morning	**soggens** [soχɛŋs]
in the afternoon	**smiddags** [smiddaχs]
in the evening	**saans** [sāŋs]

aisle seat

sitplek langs die paadjie
[sitplek laŋs di pādʒi]

window seat

venstersitplek
[fɛŋstər·sitplek]

How much?

Hoeveel?
[hufeəl?]

Can I pay by credit card?

Kan ek met 'n kredietkaart betaal?
[kan ɛk met ə kreditkārt betāl?]

Bus

bus	**bus** [bus]
intercity bus	**interstedelike bus** [interstedelikə bus]
bus stop	**bushalte** [bus·haltə]
Where's the nearest bus stop?	**Waar is die naaste bushalte?** [vār is di nāstə bus·haltə?]
number (bus ~, etc.)	**nommer** [nommər]
Which bus do I take to get to ...?	**Watter bus moet ek neem om na ... te gaan?** [vattər bus mut ɛk neəm om na ... tə χān?]
Does this bus go to ...?	**Gaan hierdie bus na ...?** [χān hirdi bus na ...?]
How frequent are the buses?	**Hoe gereëld ry die busse?** [hu χereɛlt raj di bussə?]
every 15 minutes	**elke 15 minute** [ɛlkə fajftin minutə]
every half hour	**elke half uur** [ɛlkə half ɪr]
every hour	**elke uur** [ɛlkə ɪr]
several times a day	**verskillende kere per dag** [ferskillendə kerə pər daχ]
... times a day	**... kere per dag** [... kerə pər daχ]
schedule	**diensrooster** [diŋs·roəstər]
Where can I see the schedule?	**Waar is die diensrooster?** [vār is di diŋs·roəster?]
When is the next bus?	**Wanneer vertrek die volgende bus?** [vanneər fertrek di folχendə bus?]
When is the first bus?	**Wanneer vertrek die eerste bus?** [vanneər fertrek di eərstə bus?]
When is the last bus?	**Wanneer vertrek die laaste bus?** [vanneər fertrek di lāstə bus?]

stop

next stop

last stop (terminus)

Stop here, please.

Excuse me, this is my stop.

halte
[haltə]

volgende halte
[folχendə haltə]

eindpunt
[æjnd·punt]

Stop hier, asseblief.
[stop hir, asseblif.]

Verskoon my, dis my halte.
[ferskoən maj, dis maj halte.]

Train

train	**trein** [træjn]
suburban train	**voorstedelike trein** [foərstedelikə træjn]
long-distance train	**langafstand trein** [lanχ·afstant træjn]
train station	**stasie** [stasi]
Excuse me, where is the exit to the platform?	**Verskoon my, waar is die uitgang na die perron?** [ferskoən maj, vār is di œitχaŋ na di perron?]

Does this train go to …?	**Gaan hierdie trein na …?** [χān hirdi træjn na …?]
next train	**volgende trein** [folχendə træjn]
When is the next train?	**Wanneer vertrek die volgende trein?** [vanneər fertrek di folχendə træjn?]
Where can I see the schedule?	**Waar is die diensrooster?** [vār is di diŋs·roəster?]
From which platform?	**Van watter perron?** [fan vattər perron?]
When does the train arrive in …?	**Wanneer kom die trein aan in …?** [vanneər kom di træjn ān in …?]

Please help me.	**Help my, asseblief.** [hɛlp maj, asseblif.]
I'm looking for my seat.	**Ek soek my sitplek.** [ɛk suk maj sitplek.]
We're looking for our seats.	**Ons soek ons sitplek.** [ɔŋs suk ɔŋs sitplek.]
My seat is taken.	**My sitplek is beset.** [maj sitplek is beset.]
Our seats are taken.	**Ons sitplekke is beset.** [ɔŋs sitplekkə is beset.]

I'm sorry but this is my seat.	**Jammer, dis my sitplek.** [jammər, dis maj sitplek.]
Is this seat taken?	**Is hierdie sitplek beset?** [is hirdi sitplek beset?]
May I sit here?	**Kan ek hier sit?** [kan ek hir sit?]

On the train. Dialogue (No ticket)

Ticket, please.

Kaartjie, asseblief.
[kārki, asseblif.]

I don't have a ticket.

Ek het nie 'n kaartjie nie.
[ɛk het ni ə kārki ni.]

I lost my ticket.

Ek het my kaartjie verloor.
[ɛk het maj kārki ferloər.]

I forgot my ticket at home.

Ek het my kaartjie by die huis vergeet.
[ɛk het maj kārki baj di hœis ferχeet.]

You can buy a ticket from me.

U kan 'n kaartjie van my koop.
[u kan ə kārki fan maj koəp.]

You will also have to pay a fine.

U moet 'n boete betaal.
[u mut ə butə betāl.]

Okay.

Oukei.
[æʊkæj.]

Where are you going?

Waarheen gaan u?
[vārheən χān u?]

I'm going to …

Ek gaan na …
[ɛk χān na …]

How much? I don't understand.

Hoeveel kos dit? Ek verstaan dit nie.
[hufeəl kos dit? ek ferstān dit ni.]

Write it down, please.

Skryf dit neer, asseblief.
[skrajf dit neər, asseblif.]

Okay. Can I pay with a credit card?

OK. Kan ek met 'n kredietkaart betaal?
[okej. kan ɛk met ə kreditkārt betāl?]

Yes, you can.

Ja, dit kan.
[ja, dit kan.]

Here's your receipt.

Hier is u ontvangsbewys.
[hir is u ontfaŋs·bevajs.]

Sorry about the fine.

Jammer vir die boete.
[jammər fir di bute.]

That's okay. It was my fault.

Dis oukei. Dit was my skuld.
[dis æʊkæj. dit vas maj skult.]

Enjoy your trip.

Geniet u reis.
[χenit u ræjs.]

Taxi

taxi	**taxi** [taksi]
taxi driver	**taxibestuurder** [taksi·bestɪrdər]
to catch a taxi	**'n taxi neem** [ə taksi neəm]
taxi stand	**taxistaanplek** [taksi·stānplek]
Where can I get a taxi?	**Waar kan ek 'n taxi neem?** [vār kan ɛk ə taksi neəm?]
to call a taxi	**'n taxi bel** [ə taksi bəl]
I need a taxi.	**Ek het 'n taxi nodig.** [ɛk het ə taksi nodəχ.]
Right now.	**Nou onmiddellik.** [næʊ onmiddɛllik.]
What is your address (location)?	**Wat is u adres?** [vat is u adres?]
My address is …	**My adres is …** [maj adres is …]
Your destination?	**U bestemming?** [u bestɛmmiŋ?]
Excuse me, …	**Verskoon tog, …** [ferskoən toχ, …]
Are you available?	**Is u vry?** [is u fraj?]
How much is it to get to …?	**Hoeveel kos dit na …?** [hufeəl kos dit na …?]
Do you know where it is?	**Weet u waar dit is?** [veət u vār dit is?]
Airport, please.	**Lughawe, asseblief** [luχhavə, asseblif]
Stop here, please.	**Stop hier, asseblief.** [stop hir, asseblif.]
It's not here.	**Dis nie hier nie.** [dis ni hir ni.]
This is the wrong address.	**Dis die verkeerde adres.** [dis di ferkeərdə adres.]
Turn left.	**Draai links.** [drāj links.]
Turn right.	**Draai regs.** [drāj reχs.]

How much do I owe you? | **Wat skuld ek u?**
[vat skult ek u?]

I'd like a receipt, please. | **Kan ek 'n ontvangsbewys kry, asseblief?**
[kan ek ə ontfaŋs·bevajs kraj, asseblif?]

Keep the change. | **Hou die kleingeld.**
[hæʊ di klæjɲ·xɛlt.]

Would you please wait for me? | **Sal u vir my wag, asseblief?**
[sal u fir maj vaχ, asseblif?]

five minutes | **vyf minute**
[fajf minutə]

ten minutes | **tien minute**
[tin minutə]

fifteen minutes | **vyftien minute**
[fajftin minutə]

twenty minutes | **twintig minute**
[twintəχ minutə]

half an hour | **'n halfuur**
[ə halfɪr]

Hotel

Hello.	**Hallo.** [hallo.]
My name is …	**My naam is …** [maj nām is …]
I have a reservation.	**Ek het bespreek.** [ɛk het bespreǝk.]
I need …	**Ek het … nodig** [ɛk het … nodǝχ]
a single room	**'n enkelkamer** [ǝ ɛnkǝl·kamǝr]
a double room	**'n dubbelkamer** [ǝ dubbǝl·kamǝr]
How much is that?	**Hoeveel kos dit?** [hufeǝl kos dit?]
That's a bit expensive.	**Dis nogal duur.** [dis noχal dɪr.]
Do you have anything else?	**Is daar nie ander moontlikhede nie?** [is dār ni andǝr moentlikhedǝ ni?]
I'll take it.	**Ek vat dit.** [ɛk fat dit.]
I'll pay in cash.	**Ek betaal kontant.** [ɛk betāl kontant.]
I've got a problem.	**Ek het 'n probleem.** [ɛk het ǝ probleǝm.]
My … is broken.	**My … is stukkend.** [maj … is stukkent.]
My … is out of order.	**My … is buite werking.** [maj … is bœitǝ verkiŋ.]
TV	**TV** [te·fǝ]
air conditioner	**lugreëling** [luχreɛliŋ]
tap	**kraan** [krān]
shower	**stortbad** [stortbat]
sink	**wasbak** [vasbak]
safe	**brandkas** [brant·kas]

door lock	**deur se slot** [døər sə slot]
electrical outlet	**stopkontak** [stop·kontak]
hairdryer	**haardroër** [hãr·droɛr]

I don't have ...	**Ek het nie ...** [ɛk het ni ...]
water	**water** [vatər]
light	**lig** [liχ]
electricity	**krag** [kraχ]

Can you give me ...?	**Kan u vir my ... gee?** [kan u fir maj ... χeə?]
a towel	**'n handdoek** [ə handduk]
a blanket	**'n kombers** [ə kombərs]
slippers	**pantoffels** [pantoffəls]
a robe	**'n kamerjas** [ə kamerjas]
shampoo	**sjampoe** [ʃampu]
soap	**seep** [seəp]

I'd like to change rooms.	**Ek wil van kamer verander.** [ɛk vil van kamər verandər.]
I can't find my key.	**Ek kan my sleutel nie vind nie.** [ɛk kan maj sløətəl ni fint ni.]
Could you open my room, please?	**Kan u my kamer oopsluit, asseblief?** [kan u maj kamər oəpslœit, asseblif?]
Who's there?	**Wie is daar?** [vi is dãr?]
Come in!	**Kom binne!** [kom binnə!]
Just a minute!	**'n Oomblik!** [ə oəmblik!]
Not right now, please.	**Nie nou nie, asseblief.** [ni næʊ ni, asseblif.]

Come to my room, please.	**Kom na my kamer, asseblief.** [kom na maj kamər, asseblif.]
I'd like to order food service.	**Kan ek kamerbediening kry.** [kan ɛk kamər·bediniŋ kraj.]
My room number is ...	**My kamer se nommer is ...** [maj kamər sə nommər is ...]

I'm leaving …	**Ek vertrek …** [ɛk fertrək …]
We're leaving …	**Ons vertrek …** [ɔŋs fertrek …]
right now	**nou dadellik** [næʊ dadɛllik]
this afternoon	**vanmiddag** [fanmiddaχ]
tonight	**vanaand** [fanãnt]
tomorrow	**môre** [mɔrə]
tomorrow morning	**môreoggend** [mɔrə·oχent]
tomorrow evening	**môremiddag** [mɔrə·middaχ]
the day after tomorrow	**oormôre** [oərmɔrə]

I'd like to pay.	**Ek wil betaal.** [ɛk vil betāl.]
Everything was wonderful.	**Alles was uitstekend.** [alles vas œitstekent.]
Where can I get a taxi?	**Waar kan ek 'n taxi kry?** [vār kan ɛk ə taksi kraj?]
Would you call a taxi for me, please?	**Sal u 'n taxi vir my bestel, asseblief.** [sal u ə taksi fir maj bestel, asseblif.]

Restaurant

Can I look at the menu, please? **Kan ek die spyskaart sien, asseblief?**
[kan ɛk di spajskãrt sin, asseblif?]

Table for one. **'n Tafel vir een persoon.**
[ə tafəl fir eən persoən.]

There are two (three, four) of us. **Daar is twee (drie, vier) van ons.**
[dãr is tweə (dri, fir) fan ɔŋs.]

Smoking **Rook.**
[roək.]

No smoking **Rook verbode.**
[roək ferbodə.]

Excuse me! (addressing a waiter) **Hallo! Verskoning!**
[hallo! ferskoniŋ!]

menu **spyskaart**
[spajskãrt]

wine list **wynkaart**
[vajn·kãrt]

The menu, please. **Die spyskaart, asseblief.**
[di spajskãrt, asseblif.]

Are you ready to order? **Is u gereed om te bestel?**
[is u ɣereət om tə bestel?]

What will you have? **Wat verkies u?**
[vat ferkis u?]

I'll have ... **Ek wil ... hê**
[ɛk vil ... hɛ:]

I'm a vegetarian. **Ek is vegetariër**
[ɛk is feɣetarieɾ]

meat **vleis**
[flæjs]

fish **vis**
[fis]

vegetables **groente**
[ɣruntə]

Do you have vegetarian dishes? **Het u vegetariese geregte?**
[het u feɣetarisə ɣereɣtə?]

I don't eat pork. **Ek eet nie varkvleis nie.**
[ɛk eət ni fark·flæjs ni.]

He /she/ doesn't eat meat. **Hy /sy/ eet nie vleis nie.**
[haj /saj/ eət ni flæjs ni.]

I am allergic to ... **Ek is allergies vir ...**
[ɛk is allerɣis fir ...]

Would you please bring me …

Bring vir my …, asseblief
[briŋ fir maj …, asseblif]

salt | pepper | sugar

sout | peper | suiker
[sæʊt | pepər | sœikər]

coffee | tea | dessert

koffie | tee | nagereg
[koffi | teə | naχerəχ]

water | sparkling | plain

water | bruisend | plat
[vatər | brœisent | plat]

a spoon | fork | knife

'n lepel | vurk | mes
[ə lepəl | furk | mes]

a plate | napkin

'n bord | servet
[ə bort | serfet]

Enjoy your meal!

Smaaklike ete!
[smāklikə ete!]

One more, please.

Nog een, asseblief.
[noχ eən, asseblif.]

It was very delicious.

Dit was heerlik.
[dit vas heərlik.]

check | change | tip

rekening | wisselgeld | fooitjie
[rekəniŋ | vissəlχɛlt | fojki]

Check, please.
(Could I have the check, please?)

Die rekening, asseblief.
[di rekəniŋ, asseblif.]

Can I pay by credit card?

Kan ek met 'n kredietkaart betaal?
[kan ɛk met ə kreditkārt betāl?]

I'm sorry, there's a mistake here.

Jammer, hier is 'n fout.
[jammər, hir is ə fæʊt.]

Shopping

Can I help you?	**Kan ek help?** [kan ek hɛlp?]
Do you have ...?	**Het u ...?** [het u ...?]
I'm looking for ...	**Ek soek ...** [ɛk suk ...]
I need ...	**Ek het ... nodig** [ɛk het ... nodəχ]
I'm just looking.	**Ek kyk net.** [ɛk kajk net.]
We're just looking.	**Ons kyk net.** [ɔŋs kajk net.]
I'll come back later.	**Ek kom netnou terug.** [ɛk kom netnæʊ teruχ.]
We'll come back later.	**Ons kom netnou terug.** [ɔŋs kom netnæʊ teruχ.]
discounts | sale	**afslag | uitverkoping** [afslaχ | œitferkopiŋ]
Would you please show me ...	**Kan u my ... wys, asseblief?** [kan u maj ... vajs, asseblif?]
Would you please give me ...	**Kan u my ... gee, asseblief?** [kan u maj ... χeə, asseblif?]
Can I try it on?	**Kan ek dit aanpas?** [kan ɛk dit ānpas?]
Excuse me, where's the fitting room?	**Verskoon tog, waar is die paskamer?** [ferskoən toχ, vār is di paskamer?]
Which color would you like?	**Watter kleur wil u hê?** [vattər kløər vil u hɛ:?]
size | length	**maat | lengte** [māt | leŋtə]
How does it fit?	**Pas dit?** [pas dit?]
How much is it?	**Hoeveel kos dit?** [hufeəl kos dit?]
That's too expensive.	**Dis te duur** [dis tə dɪr]
I'll take it.	**Ek sal dit vat.** [ɛk sal dit fat.]
Excuse me, where do I pay?	**Verskoon tog, waar moet ek betaal?** [ferskoən toχ, vār mut ek betāl?]

Will you pay in cash or credit card?

Betaal u kontant of met 'n kredietkaart?
[betal u kontant of met ə kreditkãrt?]

In cash | with credit card

kontant | met 'n kredietkaart
[kontant | met ə kreditkãrt]

Do you want the receipt?

Wil u 'n ontvangsbewys?
[vil u ə ontfaŋsbevajs?]

Yes, please.

Ja, asseblief.
[ja, asseblif.]

No, it's OK.

Nee, dis nie nodig nie.
[neə, dis ni nodəχ ni.]

Thank you. Have a nice day!

Dankie. Geniet die res van die dag!
[danki. χenit di res fan di daχ!]

In town

Excuse me, please.	**Verskoon tog, asseblief.** [ferskoən toχ, asseblif.]
I'm looking for …	**Ek soek …** [ɛk suk …]
the subway	**die moltrein** [di moltræjn]
my hotel	**my hotel** [maj hotəl]
the movie theater	**die bioskoop** [di bioskoəp]
a taxi stand	**'n taxistaanplek** [ə taksi·stānplek]
an ATM	**'n OTM** [ə o·te·em]
a foreign exchange office	**'n wisselkantoor** [ə vissəl·kantoər]
an internet café	**'n internetkafee** [ə internet·kafeə]
… street	**… straat** [… strāt]
this place	**hierdie plek** [hirdi plek]
Do you know where … is?	**Weet u waar … is?** [veət u vār … is?]
Which street is this?	**Watter straat is dit?** [vattər strāt is dit?]
Show me where we are right now.	**Kan u my aanwys waar ons nou is?** [kan u maj ānwajs vār ɔŋs næu is?]
Can I get there on foot?	**Kan ek soontoe stap?** [kan ek soentu stap?]
Do you have a map of the city?	**Het u 'n kaart van die stad?** [het u ə kārt fan di stat?]
How much is a ticket to get in?	**Hoeveel kos 'n toegangskaartjie?** [hufeəl kos ə tuχaŋs·kārki?]
Can I take pictures here?	**Kan ek hier foto's maak?** [kan ɛk hir fotos māk?]
Are you open?	**Is u oop?** [is u oəp?]

When do you open?   **Hoe laat gaan u oop?**
                                     [hu lāt χān u oəp?]

When do you close?   **Hoe laat sluit u?**
                                     [hu lāt slœit u?]

Money

money	**geld** [χεlt]
cash	**kontant** [kontant]
paper money	**bankbiljette** [bank·biljεttə]
loose change	**kleingeld** [klæjn·χεlt]
check | change | tip	**rekening | wisselgeld | fooitjie** [rekəniŋ | vissəlχεlt | fojki]
credit card	**kredietkaart** [kreditkãrt]
wallet	**beursie** [bøərsi]
to buy	**koop** [koəp]
to pay	**betaal** [betãl]
fine	**boete** [butə]
free	**gratis** [χratis]
Where can I buy ...?	**Waar kan ek ... koop?** [vãr kan εk ... koəp?]
Is the bank open now?	**Is die bank nou oop?** [is di bank næʊ oəp?]
When does it open?	**Wanneer maak dit oop?** [vanneər mãk dit oəp?]
When does it close?	**Wanneer maak dit toe?** [vanneər mãk dit tu?]
How much?	**Hoeveel?** [hufeəl?]
How much is this?	**Hoeveel kos dit?** [hufeəl kos dit?]
That's too expensive.	**Dis te duur.** [dis tə dɪr.]
Excuse me, where do I pay?	**Verskoon tog, waar moet ek betaal?** [ferskoən toχ, vãr mut ek betãl?]
Check, please.	**Die rekening, asseblief.** [di rekəniŋ, asseblif.]

Can I pay by credit card? | **Kan ek met 'n kredietkaart betaal?**
[kan ɛk met ə kreditkãrt betãl?]

Is there an ATM here? | **Verskoon tog, is hier 'n OTM?**
[ferskoən toχ, is hir ə o·te·em?]

I'm looking for an ATM. | **Ek soek 'n OTM.**
[ɛk suk ə o·te·em.]

I'm looking for a foreign exchange office. | **Ek soek 'n wisselkantoor.**
[ɛk suk ə vissəl·kantoər.]

I'd like to change … | **Ek sou … wou wissel.**
[ɛk sæʋ … væʋ vissəl.]

What is the exchange rate? | **Wat is die wisselkoers?**
[vat is di vissəlkurs?]

Do you need my passport? | **Het u my paspoort nodig?**
[het u maj paspoərt nodəχ?]

Time

What time is it?	**Hoe laat is dit?** [hu lāt is dit?]
When?	**Wanneer?** [vanneər?]
At what time?	**Hoe laat?** [hu lāt?]
now | later | after …	**nou | later | na …** [næʊ | latər | na …]
one o'clock	**een uur** [eən ɪr]
one fifteen	**kwart oor een** [kwart oər eən]
one thirty	**half twee** [half tweə]
one forty-five	**kwart voor twee** [kwart foər tweə]
one | two | three	**een | twee | drie** [eən | tweə | dri]
four | five | six	**vier | vyf | ses** [fir | fajf | ses]
seven | eight | nine	**sewe | ag | nege** [sevə | aχ | neχə]
ten | eleven | twelve	**tien | elf | twaalf** [tin | ɛlf | twālf]
in …	**binne …** [binnə …]
five minutes	**vyf minute** [fajf minutə]
ten minutes	**tien minute** [tin minutə]
fifteen minutes	**vyftien minute** [fajftin minutə]
twenty minutes	**twintig minute** [twintəχ minutə]
half an hour	**'n halfuur** [ə halfɪr]
an hour	**'n uur** [ə ɪr]

in the morning	**soggens** [soxɛŋs]
early in the morning	**soggens vroeg** [soxɛŋs frux]
this morning	**vanoggend** [fanoxent]
tomorrow morning	**môreoggend** [mɔrə·oxent]
in the middle of the day	**in die middel van die dag** [in di middəl fan di dax]
in the afternoon	**smiddags** [smiddaxs]
in the evening	**saans** [sãŋs]
tonight	**vanaand** [fanãnt]
at night	**saans** [sãŋs]
yesterday	**gister** [xistər]
today	**vandag** [fandax]
tomorrow	**môre** [mɔrə]
the day after tomorrow	**oormôre** [oərmɔrə]
What day is it today?	**Watter dag is dit vandag?** [vattər dax is dit fandax?]
It's …	**Dit is …** [dit is …]
Monday	**maandag** [mãndax]
Tuesday	**dinsdag** [dinsdax]
Wednesday	**woensdag** [voɛŋsdax]
Thursday	**Donderdag** [dondərdax]
Friday	**vrydag** [frajdax]
Saturday	**saterdag** [satərdax]
Sunday	**sondag** [sondax]

Greetings. Introductions

Hello.
Hallo.
[hallo.]

Pleased to meet you.
Aangename kennis.
[ānχәnamә kɛnnis.]

Me too.
Dieselfde.
[disɛlfdә.]

I'd like you to meet …
Kan ek jou voorstel aan …
[kan ɛk jæʊ foәrstәl ān …]

Nice to meet you.
Aangename kennis.
[ānχәnamә kɛnnis.]

How are you?
Hoe gaan dit?
[hu χān dit?]

My name is …
My naam is …
[maj nām is …]

His name is …
Dis …
[dis …]

Her name is …
Dis …
[dis …]

What's your name?
Wat is u naam?
[vat is u nām?]

What's his name?
Wat is sy naam?
[vat is saj nām?]

What's her name?
Wat is haar naam?
[vat is hār nām?]

What's your last name?
Wat is u van?
[vat is u fan?]

You can call me …
Noem my maar …
[num maj mār …]

Where are you from?
Vanwaar kom u?
[fanwār kom u?]

I'm from …
Ek kom van …
[ɛk kom fan …]

What do you do for a living?
Wat is u beroep?
[vat is u berup?]

Who is this?
Wie is dit?
[vi is dit?]

Who is he?
Wie is hy?
[vi is haj?]

Who is she?
Wie is sy?
[vi is saj?]

Who are they?
Wie is hulle?
[vi is hullә?]

This is …

Dit is …
[dit is …]

my friend (masc.)

my vriend
[maj frint]

my friend (fem.)

my vriendin
[maj frindin]

my husband

my man
[maj man]

my wife

my vrou
[maj fræʊ]

my father

my vader
[maj fadər]

my mother

my moeder
[maj mudər]

my brother

my broer
[maj brur]

my son

my seun
[maj søən]

my daughter

my dogter
[maj doχtər]

This is our son.

Dit is ons seun.
[dit is ɔŋs søən.]

This is our daughter.

Dit is ons dogter.
[dit is ɔŋs doχter.]

These are my children.

Dit is my kinders.
[dit is maj kindərs.]

These are our children.

Dit is ons kinders.
[dit is ɔŋs kindərs.]

Farewells

Good bye!

Totsiens!
[totsiŋs!]

Bye! (inform.)

Koebaai!
[kubãi!]

See you tomorrow.

Sien jou môre.
[sin jæʊ mɔrə.]

See you soon.

Totsiens.
[totsiŋs.]

See you at seven.

Sien jou om sewe uur.
[sin jæʊ om sevə ɪr.]

Have fun!

Geniet dit!
[χenit dit!]

Talk to you later.

Gesels later.
[χesɛls latər.]

Have a nice weekend.

Geniet die naweek.
[χenit di naveək.]

Good night.

Lekker slaap.
[lɛkkər slãp.]

It's time for me to go.

Dis tyd om te gaan.
[dis tajt om tə χãn.]

I have to go.

Ek moet loop.
[ɛk mut loəp.]

I will be right back.

Ek is nounou terug.
[ɛk is næʊnæʊ teruχ.]

It's late.

Dis al laat.
[dis al lãt.]

I have to get up early.

Ek moet vroeg opstaan.
[ɛk mut fruχ opstãn.]

I'm leaving tomorrow.

Ek vertrek môre.
[ɛk fertrək mɔrə.]

We're leaving tomorrow.

Ons vertrek môre.
[ɔŋs fertrek mɔrə.]

Have a nice trip!

Geniet die reis!
[χenit di ræjs!]

It was nice meeting you.

Ek het dit geniet om jou te ontmoet.
[ɛk het dit χenit om jæʊ tə ontmut.]

It was nice talking to you.

Dit was lekker om met jou te gesels.
[dit vas lɛkkər om met jæʊ tə χesɛls.]

Thanks for everything.

Baie dankie vir alles.
[baje danki fir alles.]

I had a very good time.

Ek het dit geniet.
[ɛk het dit χenit.]

We had a very good time.

Ons het dit baie geniet.
[ɔŋs het dit baje χenit.]

It was really great.

Dit was regtig oulik.
[dit vas reχteχ æʊlik.]

I'm going to miss you.

Ek gaan jou mis.
[ɛk χān jæʊ mis.]

We're going to miss you.

Ons gaan jou mis.
[ɔŋs χān jæʊ mis.]

Good luck!

Sukses!
[suksɛs!]

Say hi to …

Stuur groete vir …
[stɪr χrutə fir …]

Foreign language

I don't understand.	**Ek verstaan dit nie.** [ɛk ferstãn dit ni.]
Write it down, please.	**Skryf dit neer, asseblief.** [skrajf dit neər, asseblif.]
Do you speak ...?	**Praat u ...?** [prãt u ...?]
I speak a little bit of ...	**Ek praat 'n bietjie ...** [ɛk prãt ə biki ...]
English	**Engels** [ɛŋəls]
Turkish	**Turks** [turks]
Arabic	**Arabies** [arabis]
French	**Frans** [fraŋs]
German	**Duits** [dœits]
Italian	**Italiaans** [italiãŋs]
Spanish	**Spaans** [spãŋs]
Portuguese	**Portugees** [portuχeəs]
Chinese	**Sjinees** [ʃineəs]
Japanese	**Japannees** [japanneəs]
Can you repeat that, please.	**Kan u dit herhaal asseblief** [kan u dit herhãl asseblif]
I understand.	**Ek verstaan dit.** [ɛk ferstãn dit.]
I don't understand.	**Ek verstaan dit nie.** [ɛk ferstãn dit ni.]
Please speak more slowly.	**Praat bietjie stadiger asseblief.** [prãt biki stadiχər asseblif.]
Is that correct? (Am I saying it right?)	**Is dit reg?** [is dit reχ?]
What is this? (What does this mean?)	**Wat is dit?** [vat is dit?]

Apologies

Excuse me, please.	**Verskoon my, asseblief.** [ferskoən maj, asseblif.]
I'm sorry.	**Jammer.** [jammər.]
I'm really sorry.	**Ek is baie jammer.** [ɛk is baje jammər.]
Sorry, it's my fault.	**Jammer, dis my skuld.** [jammər, dis maj skult.]
My mistake.	**My skuld.** [maj skult.]

May I ...?	**Mag ek ...?** [maχ ek ...?]
Do you mind if I ...?	**Sal u omgee as ek ...?** [sal u omχeə as ek ...?]
It's OK.	**Dis OK.** [dis okej.]
It's all right.	**Maak nie saak nie.** [māk ni sāk ni.]
Don't worry about it.	**Moet jou nie daaroor bekommer nie.** [mut jæʋ ni dāroər bekommər ni.]

Agreement

Yes.	**Ja.** [ja.]
Yes, sure.	**Ja, beslis.** [ja, beslis.]
OK (Good!)	**OK. Goed!** [okej. χut!]
Very well.	**Uitstekend.** [œitstekent]
Certainly!	**Definitief!** [definitif!]
I agree.	**Ek stem saam.** [ɛk stem sãm.]
That's correct.	**Dis reg.** [dis reχ.]
That's right.	**Dis reg.** [dis reχ.]
You're right.	**U is reg.** [u is reχ.]
I don't mind.	**Ek gee nie om nie.** [ɛk χeə ni om ni.]
Absolutely right.	**Heeltemal reg.** [heəltemal reχ.]
It's possible.	**Dis moontlik.** [dis moentlik.]
That's a good idea.	**Dis 'n goeie idee.** [dis ə χuje ideə.]
I can't say no.	**Ek kan nie nee sê nie.** [ɛk kan ni neə sɛ: ni.]
I'd be happy to.	**Dis 'n plesier.** [dis ə plesir.]
With pleasure.	**Plesier.** [plesir.]

Refusal. Expressing doubt

No.	**Nee** [neə]
Certainly not.	**Beslis nie.** [beslis ni.]
I don't agree.	**Ek stem nie saam nie.** [ɛk stem ni sãm ni.]
I don't think so.	**Ek glo dit nie.** [ɛk χlo dit ni.]
It's not true.	**Dis nie waar nie.** [dis ni vãr ni.]
You are wrong.	**U maak 'n fout.** [u mãk ə fæʊt.]
I think you are wrong.	**Ek dink u is verkeerd.** [ɛk dink u is ferkeərt.]
I'm not sure.	**Ek is nie seker nie.** [ɛk is ni sekər ni.]
It's impossible.	**Dis onmoontlik.** [dis onmoentlik.]
Nothing of the kind (sort)!	**Glad nie!** [χlat ni!]
The exact opposite.	**Net die teenoorgestelde!** [net di teənoərχestɛlde!]
I'm against it.	**Ek is daarteen.** [ɛk is dãrteən.]
I don't care.	**Ek gee nie om nie.** [ɛk χeə ni om ni.]
I have no idea.	**Ek het nie 'n idee nie.** [ɛk het ni ə ideə ni.]
I doubt it.	**Ek betwyfel dit.** [ɛk betwajfəl dit.]
Sorry, I can't.	**Jammer, ek kan nie.** [jammər, ɛk kan ni.]
Sorry, I don't want to.	**Jammer, ek wil nie.** [jammər, ɛk vil ni.]
Thank you, but I don't need this.	**Dankie, maar ek het dit nie nodig nie.** [danki, mãr ɛk het dit ni nodəχ ni.]
It's getting late.	**Dit word laat.** [dit vort lãt.]

I have to get up early.   **Ek moet vroeg opstaan.**
                                   [ɛk mut fruχ opstān.]

I don't feel well.   **Ek voel nie lekker nie.**
                                   [ɛk ful ni lɛkkər ni.]

Expressing gratitude

Thank you.	**Baie dankie.** [baje danki.]
Thank you very much.	**Baie dankie.** [baje danki.]
I really appreciate it.	**Ek waardeer dit.** [ɛk vārdeər dit.]
I'm really grateful to you.	**Ek is u baie dankbaar.** [ɛk is u baje dankbār.]
We are really grateful to you.	**Ons is u baie dankbaar.** [ɔŋs is u baje dankbār.]

Thank you for your time.	**Baie dankie vir u tyd.** [baje danki fir u tajt.]
Thanks for everything.	**Baie dankie vir alles.** [baje danki fir alles.]
Thank you for ...	**Dankie vir ...** [danki fir ...]
your help	**u hulp** [u hulp]
a nice time	**vir 'n lekker tydjie** [fir ə lɛkkər tajdʒi]

a wonderful meal	**'n heerlike ete** [ə heərlikə etə]
a pleasant evening	**'n aangename aand** [ə ānχənamə ānt]
a wonderful day	**'n oulike dag** [ə æulikə daχ]
an amazing journey	**'n wonderlike reis** [ə vondərlikə ræjs]

Don't mention it.	**Plesier.** [plesir.]
You are welcome.	**Plesier.** [plesir.]
Any time.	**Enige tyd.** [ɛniχə tajt.]
My pleasure.	**Plesier.** [plesir.]
Forget it.	**Plesier.** [plesir.]
Don't worry about it.	**Moet jou nie bekommer nie.** [mut jæu ni bekommər ni.]

Congratulations. Best wishes

Congratulations!

Geluk!
[χeluk!]

Happy birthday!

Geluk met jou verjaardag!
[χeluk met jæu ferjārdaχ!]

Merry Christmas!

Geseënde Kersfees!
[χeseɛndə kersfeɛs!]

Happy New Year!

Gelukkige Nuwejaar!
[χelukkiχə nuvejār!]

Happy Easter!

Geseënde Paasfees!
[χeseɛndə pāsfeɛs!]

Happy Hanukkah!

Gelukkige Chanoeka!
[χelukkiχə χanuka!]

I'd like to propose a toast.

Ek wil graag 'n heildronk instel.
[ɛk vil χrāχ ə hæjldronk instəl.]

Cheers!

Gesondheid!
[χesonthæjt!]

Let's drink to …!

Laat ons drink op …!
[lāt ɔŋs drink op …!]

To our success!

Op jou sukses!
[op jæu suksɛs!]

To your success!

Op u sukses!
[op u suksɛs!]

Good luck!

Sukses!
[suksɛs!]

Have a nice day!

Geniet die dag!
[χenit di daχ!]

Have a good holiday!

Geniet die vakansie!
[χenit di fakaŋsi!]

Have a safe journey!

Veilig ry!
[fæjləχ raj!]

I hope you get better soon!

Ek hoop u voel gou beter!
[ɛk hoəp u fʉl χæu beter!]

Socializing

Why are you sad?

Hoekom lyk u so droewig?
[hukom lajk u so druvɛχ?]

Smile! Cheer up!

Lag 'n bietjie! Wees vrolik!
[laχ ə biki! veəs frolik!]

Are you free tonight?

Is u vry vanaand?
[is u fraj fanãnt?]

May I offer you a drink?

Kan ek 'n drankie vir jou kry?
[kan ek ə dranki fir jæʊ kraj?]

Would you like to dance?

Wil u dans?
[vil u daŋs?]

Let's go to the movies.

Sal ons bioskoop toe gaan?
[sal ɔŋs bioskoəp tu χãn?]

May I invite you to ...?

Mag ek jou uitnooi na ...?
[maχ ek jæʊ œitnoj na ...?]

a restaurant

'n restaurant
[ə restɔurant]

the movies

die bioskoop
[di bioskoəp]

the theater

die teater
[di teatər]

go for a walk

gaan stap
[χãn stap]

At what time?

Hoe laat?
[hu lãt?]

tonight

vanaand
[fanãnt]

at six

om ses uur
[om ses ɪr]

at seven

om sewe uur
[om sevə ɪr]

at eight

om agt uur
[om aχt ɪr]

at nine

om nege uur
[om neχə ɪr]

Do you like it here?

Geniet u dit hier?
[χenit u dit hir?]

Are you here with someone?

Is u hier saam met iemand?
[is u hir sãm met imant?]

I'm with my friend.

Ek is met my vriend.
[ɛk is met maj frint.]

I'm with my friends.

Ek is met my vriende.
[ɛk is met maj frində.]

No, I'm alone.

Nee, ek is alleen.
[neə, ek is alleən.]

Do you have a boyfriend?

Het jy 'n kêrel?
[het jaj ə kærel?]

I have a boyfriend.

Ek het 'n kêrel.
[ɛk het ə kærel.]

Do you have a girlfriend?

Het jy 'n meisie?
[het jaj ə mæjsi?]

I have a girlfriend.

Ek het 'n meisie.
[ɛk het ə mæjsi.]

Can I see you again?

Kan ek jou weer sien?
[kan ek jæʊ veər sin?]

Can I call you?

Kan ek jou bel?
[kan ek jæʊ bel?]

Call me. (Give me a call.)

Bel my.
[bel maj.]

What's your number?

Wat is jou nommer?
[vat is jæʊ nommər?]

I miss you.

Ek mis jou.
[ɛk mis jæʊ.]

You have a beautiful name.

U het 'n mooi naam.
[u het ə moj nām.]

I love you.

Ek hou van jou.
[ɛk hæʊ fan jæʊ.]

Will you marry me?

Wil jy met my trou?
[vil jaj met maj træʊ?]

You're kidding!

U maak grappies!
[u māk χrappis!]

I'm just kidding.

Ek maak net 'n grappie.
[ɛk māk net ə χrappi.]

Are you serious?

Bedoel u dit?
[bedul u dit?]

I'm serious.

Ek is ernstig.
[ɛk is ernstəχ.]

Really?!

Regtig waar?!
[reχtəχ vār?!]

It's unbelievable!

Dis ongelooflik.
[dis onχeloəflik.]

I don't believe you.

Ek glo jou nie.
[ɛk χlo jæʊ ni.]

I can't.

Ek kan nie.
[ɛk kan ni.]

I don't know.

Ek weet dit nie.
[ɛk veət dit ni.]

I don't understand you.

Ek verstaan u nie.
[ɛk ferstān u ni.]

Please go away.

Loop asseblief.
[loəp asseblif.]

Leave me alone!

Los my uit!
[los maj œit!]

I can't stand him.

Ek kan hom nie verdra nie.
[ɛk kan hom ni ferdra ni.]

You are disgusting!

U is walglik!
[u is valχlik!]

I'll call the police!

Ek gaan die polisie bel!
[ɛk χān di polisi bel!]

Sharing impressions. Emotions

I like it.
Ek hou daarvan.
[ɛk hæʊ dārfan.]

Very nice.
Baie mooi.
[baje moj.]

That's great!
Dis oulik!
[dis æʊlik!]

It's not bad.
Dis nie sleg nie.
[dis ni sleχ ni.]

I don't like it.
Ek hou nie daarvan nie.
[ɛk hæʊ ni dārfan ni.]

It's not good.
Dis nie goed nie.
[dis ni χut ni.]

It's bad.
Dis sleg.
[dis sleχ.]

It's very bad.
Dis baie sleg.
[dis baje sleχ.]

It's disgusting.
Dis walglik.
[dis valχlik.]

I'm happy.
Ek is bly.
[ɛk is blaj.]

I'm content.
Ek is tevrede.
[ɛk is tefrede.]

I'm in love.
Ek is verlief.
[ɛk is ferlif.]

I'm calm.
Ek is rustig.
[ɛk is rustəχ.]

I'm bored.
Ek verveel my.
[ɛk ferfeəl maj.]

I'm tired.
Ek is moeg.
[ɛk is muχ.]

I'm sad.
Ek is droewig.
[ɛk is druvəχ.]

I'm frightened.
Ek is bang.
[ɛk is baŋ.]

I'm angry.
Ek is kwaad.
[ɛk is kwāt.]

I'm worried.
Ek is bekommerd.
[ɛk is bekommert.]

I'm nervous.
Ek is senuweeagtig.
[ɛk is senuveə aχtəχ.]

I'm jealous. (envious)

Ek is jaloers.
[εk is jalurs.]

I'm surprised.

Dit verbaas my.
[dit ferbãs maj.]

I'm perplexed.

Ek is verbouereerd.
[εk is ferbæʊreərt.]

Problems. Accidents

I've got a problem.	**Ek het 'n probleem.** [ɛk het ə probleəm.]
We've got a problem.	**Ons het 'n probleem.** [ɔŋs het ə probleəm.]
I'm lost.	**Ek het verdwaal.** [ɛk het ferdwāl.]
I missed the last bus (train).	**Ek het die laaste bus (trein) gemis.** [ɛk het di lāstə bus (træjn) χemis.]
I don't have any money left.	**My geld is op.** [maj χɛlt is op.]

I've lost my ...	**Ek het my ... verloor** [ɛk het maj ... ferloər]
Someone stole my ...	**Lemand het my ... gesteel.** [lemant het maj ... χesteəl.]
passport	**paspoort** [paspoərt]
wallet	**beursie** [bøərsi]
papers	**papiere** [papirə]
ticket	**kaartjie** [kārki]

money	**geld** [χɛlt]
handbag	**handsak** [hand·sak]
camera	**kamera** [kamera]
laptop	**skootrekenaar** [skoət·rekənār]
tablet computer	**tablet** [tablet]
mobile phone	**selfoon** [sɛlfoən]

Help me!	**Help!** [hɛlp!]
What's happened?	**Wat's fout?** [vats fæʊt?]
fire	**brand** [brant]

shooting	**daar word geskiet** [dãr vort χeskit]
murder	**moord** [moərt]
explosion	**ontploffing** [ontploffiŋ]
fight	**geveg** [χefeχ]

Call the police!	**Bel die polisie!** [bel di polisi!]
Please hurry up!	**Maak gou asseblief!** [mãk χæʊ asseblif!]
I'm looking for the police station.	**Ek soek die polisiekantoor.** [ɛk suk di polisi·kantoər.]
I need to make a call.	**Ek moet bel.** [ɛk mut bel.]
May I use your phone?	**Mag ek u telefoon gebruik?** [maχ ek u telefoən χebrœik?]

I've been …	**Ek is …** [ɛk is …]
mugged	**aangeval** [ãnχəfal]
robbed	**beroof** [beroəf]
raped	**verkrag** [ferkraχ]
attacked (beaten up)	**aangeval** [ãnχəfal]

Are you all right?	**Gaan dit?** [χãn dit?]
Did you see who it was?	**Het u gesien wie dit was?** [het u χesin vi dit vas?]
Would you be able to recognize the person?	**Sou u die persoon kon herken?** [sæʊ u di persoən kon herken?]
Are you sure?	**Is u seker?** [is u seker?]

Please calm down.	**Kom tot bedaring asseblief.** [kom tot bedariŋ asseblif.]
Take it easy!	**Rustig!** [rustəχ!]
Don't worry!	**Moenie bekommerd wees nie!** [muni bekommert veəs ni!]
Everything will be fine.	**Alles sal reg kom.** [alles sal reχ kom.]
Everything's all right.	**Alles is reg.** [alles is reχ.]
Come here, please.	**Kom hier asseblief.** [kom hir asseblif.]

I have some questions for you.

Ek het 'n paar vrae vir u.
[ɛk het ə pãr fraə fir u.]

Wait a moment, please.

Wag 'n bietjie, asseblief.
[vaχ ə biki, asseblif.]

Do you have any I.D.?

Het u 'n identiteitskaart?
[het u ə identitæjts·kãrt?]

Thanks. You can leave now.

Dankie. U kan nou loop.
[danki. u kan næʊ loəp.]

Hands behind your head!

Hande agter jou kop!
[handə aχtər jæʊ kop!]

You're under arrest!

U is onder arres!
[u is ondər arres!]

Health problems

Please help me.

Help my, asseblief.
[hɛlp maj, asseblif.]

I don't feel well.

Ek voel nie lekker nie.
[ɛk ful ni lɛkkər ni.]

My husband doesn't feel well.

My man voel nie lekker nie.
[maj man ful ni lɛkkər ni.]

My son ...

My seun ...
[maj søən ...]

My father ...

My pa ...
[maj pa ...]

My wife doesn't feel well.

My vrou voel nie lekker nie.
[maj fræʊ ful ni lɛkkər ni.]

My daughter ...

My dogter ...
[maj doχtər ...]

My mother ...

My ma ...
[maj ma ...]

I've got a ...

Ek het ...
[ɛk het ...]

headache

koppyn
[koppajn]

sore throat

keelpyn
[keəl·pajn]

stomach ache

maagpyn
[māχpajn]

toothache

tandpyn
[tand·pajn]

I feel dizzy.

Ek voel duiselig.
[ɛk ful dœiseləχ.]

He has a fever.

Hy het koors.
[haj het koərs.]

She has a fever.

Sy het koors.
[saj het koərs.]

I can't breathe.

Ek kan nie goed asemhaal nie.
[ɛk kan ni χut asemhāl ni.]

I'm short of breath.

Ek is kortasem.
[ɛk is kortasem.]

I am asthmatic.

Ek is asmaties.
[ɛk is asmatis.]

I am diabetic.

Ek is diabeet.
[ɛk is diabeət.]

I can't sleep.	**Ek kan nie slaap nie.** [ɛk kan ni slāp ni.]
food poisoning	**voedselvergiftiging** [fudsəl·ferχiftəχiŋ]

It hurts here.	**Dis seer hier.** [dis seər hir.]
Help me!	**Help!** [hɛlp!]
I am here!	**Ek is hier!** [ɛk is hir!]
We are here!	**Ons is hier!** [oŋs is hir!]
Get me out of here!	**Kom kry my!** [kom kraj maj!]
I need a doctor.	**Ek het 'n dokter nodig.** [ɛk het ə doktər nodəχ.]
I can't move.	**Ek kan nie beweeg nie.** [ɛk kan ni beveəχ ni.]
I can't move my legs.	**Ek kan my bene nie beweeg nie.** [ɛk kan maj benə ni beveəχ ni.]

I have a wound.	**Ek het 'n wond.** [ɛk het ə vont.]
Is it serious?	**Is dit ernstig?** [is dit ernstəχ?]
My documents are in my pocket.	**My dokumente is in my sak.** [maj dokumentə is in maj sak.]
Calm down!	**Bedaar!** [bedār!]
May I use your phone?	**Mag ek u telefoon gebruik?** [maχ ek u telefoən χebrœik?]

Call an ambulance!	**Bel 'n ambulans!** [bel ə ambulaŋs!]
It's urgent!	**Dis dringend!** [dis driŋənd!]
It's an emergency!	**Dis 'n noodgeval!** [dis ə noədχefal!]
Please hurry up!	**Maak gou asseblief!** [māk χæʊ asseblif!]
Would you please call a doctor?	**Kan u asseblief 'n dokter bel?** [kan u asseblif ə doktər bel?]
Where is the hospital?	**Waar is die hospitaal?** [vār is di hospitāl?]

How are you feeling?	**Hoe voel u?** [hu ful u?]
Are you all right?	**Hoe gaan dit?** [hu χān dit?]
What's happened?	**Wat het gebeur?** [vat het χebøər?]

I feel better now.

Ek voel nou beter.
[ɛk ful næʊ betər.]

It's OK.

Dis OK.
[dis okej.]

It's all right.

Dit gaan goed.
[dit χān χut.]

At the pharmacy

pharmacy (drugstore)	**apteek** [apteək]
24-hour pharmacy	**24 uur apteek** [fir-en-twintəχ ɪr apteək]
Where is the closest pharmacy?	**Waar is die naaste apteek?** [vār is di nāstə apteək?]
Is it open now?	**Is hy nou oop?** [is haj næʊ oəp?]
At what time does it open?	**Hoe laat gaan hy oop?** [hu lāt χān haj oəp?]
At what time does it close?	**Hoe laat sluit hy?** [hu lāt slœit haj?]
Is it far?	**Is dit ver?** [is dit fer?]
Can I get there on foot?	**Kan ek soontoe stap?** [kan ek soentu stap?]
Can you show me on the map?	**Kan u dit op die stadskaart aanwys?** [kan u dit op di statskārt ānwajs?]
Please give me something for ...	**Gee my iets vir ... asseblief** [χeə maj its fir ... asseblif]
a headache	**koppyn** [koppajn]
a cough	**hoes** [hus]
a cold	**verkoudheid** [ferkæʊdhæjt]
the flu	**griep** [χrip]
a fever	**koors** [koərs]
a stomach ache	**maagpyn** [māχpajn]
nausea	**naarheid** [nārhæjt]
diarrhea	**diarree** [diarreə]
constipation	**konstipasie** [koŋstipasi]
pain in the back	**rugpyn** [ruχpajn]

chest pain — **borspyn**
[borspajn]

side stitch — **steek in my sy**
[steək in maj saj]

abdominal pain — **pyn in my onderbuik**
[pajn in maj ondərbœik]

pill — **pil**
[pil]

ointment, cream — **salf, room**
[salf, roəm]

syrup — **stroop**
[stroəp]

spray — **sproeier**
[sprujer]

drops — **druppels**
[druppɛls]

You need to go to the hospital. — **U moet hospitaal toe gaan.**
[u mut hospitāl tu χān.]

health insurance — **siekteversekering**
[siktə·fersekeriŋ]

prescription — **voorskrif**
[foərskrif]

insect repellant — **insekmiddel**
[insek·middəl]

Band Aid — **kleefverband**
[kleəffər·bant]

The bare minimum

Excuse me, ...	**Verskoon my, ...** [ferskoən maj, ...]
Hello.	**Hallo.** [hallo.]
Thank you.	**Baie dankie.** [baje danki.]
Good bye.	**Totsiens.** [totsiŋs.]
Yes.	**Ja.** [ja.]
No.	**Nee.** [neə.]
I don't know.	**Ek weet nie.** [ɛk veət ni.]
Where? | Where to? | When?	**Waar? | Waarheen? | Wanneer?** [vār? | vārheən? | vanneər?]

I need ...	**Ek het ... nodig** [ɛk het ... nodəχ]
I want ...	**Ek wil ...** [ɛk vil ...]
Do you have ...?	**Het u ...?** [het u ...?]
Is there a ... here?	**Is hier 'n ...?** [is hir ə ...?]
May I ...?	**Mag ek ...?** [maχ ek ...?]
..., please (polite request)	**... asseblief** [... asseblif]

I'm looking for ...	**Ek soek ...** [ɛk suk ...]
restroom	**toilet** [tojlet]
ATM	**OTM** [o·te·em]
pharmacy (drugstore)	**apteek** [apteək]
hospital	**hospitaal** [hospitāl]
police station	**polisiekantoor** [polisi·kantoər]
subway	**moltrein** [moltræjn]

| taxi | **taxi**
[taksi] |
| train station | **stasie**
[stasi] |

My name is …	**My naam is …** [maj nãm is …]
What's your name?	**Wat is u naam?** [vat is u nãm?]
Could you please help me?	**Kan u my help, asseblief?** [kan u maj hɛlp, asseblif?]
I've got a problem.	**Ek het 'n probleem.** [ɛk het ə probleəm.]
I don't feel well.	**Ek voel nie lekker nie.** [ɛk ful ni lɛkkər ni.]
Call an ambulance!	**Bel 'n ambulans!** [bel ə ambulaŋs!]
May I make a call?	**Kan ek 'n oproep maak?** [kan ɛk ə oprup mãk?]

| I'm sorry. | **Jammer.**
[jammər.] |
| You're welcome. | **Plesier.**
[plesir.] |

I, me	**Ek, my** [ek, maj]
you (inform.)	**jy** [jaj]
he	**hy** [haj]
she	**sy** [saj]
they (masc.)	**hulle** [hullə]
they (fem.)	**hulle** [hullə]
we	**ons** [ɔŋs]
you (pl)	**julle** [jullə]
you (sg, form.)	**u** [u]

ENTRANCE	**INGANG** [inχaŋ]
EXIT	**UITGANG** [œitχaŋ]
OUT OF ORDER	**BUITE WERKING** [bœitə verkiŋ]
CLOSED	**GESLUIT** [χeslœit]

OPEN

OOP
[oəp]

FOR WOMEN

DAMES
[dames]

FOR MEN

MANS
[maŋs]

TOPICAL VOCABULARY

This section contains more than 3,000 of the most important words.
The dictionary will provide invaluable assistance while traveling abroad, because frequently individual words are enough for you to be understood.
The dictionary includes a convenient transcription of each foreign word

T&P Books Publishing

VOCABULARY
CONTENTS

T&P Books Publishing

BASIC CONCEPTS

T&P Books Publishing

1. Pronouns

I, me	ek, my	[ɛk], [maj]
you	jy	[jaj]
he	hy	[haj]
she	sy	[saj]
it	dit	[dit]
we	ons	[ɔŋs]
you (to a group)	julle	[jullə]
you (polite, sing.)	u	[u]
you (polite, pl)	u	[u]
they	hulle	[hullə]

2. Greetings. Salutations

Hello! (fam.)	**Hallo!**	[hallo!]
Hello! (form.)	**Hallo!**	[hallo!]
Good morning!	**Goeie môre!**	[χuje mɔrə!]
Good afternoon!	**Goeiemiddag!**	[χuje·middaχ!]
Good evening!	**Goeienaand!**	[χuje·nānt!]
to say hello	**dagsê**	[daχsɛ:]
Hi! (hello)	**Hallo!**	[hallo!]
greeting (n)	**groet**	[χrut]
to greet (vt)	**groet**	[χrut]
How are you?	**Hoe gaan dit?**	[hu χān dit?]
What's new?	**Hoe gaan dit?**	[hu χān dit?]
Goodbye!	**Totsiens!**	[totsiŋs!]
Bye!	**Koebaai!**	[kubāi!]
See you soon!	**Totsiens!**	[totsiŋs!]
Farewell!	**Totsiens!**	[totsiŋs!]
Farewell! (to a friend)	**Mooi loop!**	[moj loəp!]
Farewell! (form.)	**Vaarwel!**	[fārwel!]
to say goodbye	**afskeid neem**	[afskæjt neəm]
So long!	**Koebaai!**	[kubāi!]
Thank you!	**Dankie!**	[danki!]
Thank you very much!	**Baie dankie!**	[baje danki!]
You're welcome.	**Plesier.**	[plesir]
Don't mention it.	**Plesier.**	[plesir]
It was nothing.	**Plesier.**	[plesir]

Excuse me! (fam.)	**Ekskuus!**	[ɛkskɪs!]
Excuse me! (form.)	**Verskoon my!**	[ferskoən maj!]
to excuse (forgive)	**verskoon**	[ferskoən]

to apologize (vi)	**verskoning vra**	[ferskoniŋ fra]
My apologies	**Verskoning**	[ferskoniŋ]
I'm sorry!	**Ek is jammer!**	[ɛk is jammər!]
to forgive (vt)	**vergewe**	[ferχevə]
It's okay! (that's all right)	**Maak nie saak nie!**	[māk ni sāk ni!]
please (adv)	**asseblief**	[asseblif]

Don't forget!	**Vergeet dit nie!**	[ferχeət dit ni!]
Certainly!	**Beslis!**	[beslis!]
Of course not!	**Natuurlik nie!**	[natɪrlik ni!]
Okay! (I agree)	**OK!**	[okej!]
That's enough!	**Dis genoeg!**	[dis χenuχ!]

3. Questions

Who?	**Wie?**	[vi?]
What?	**Wat?**	[vat?]
Where? (at, in)	**Waar?**	[vār?]
Where (to)?	**Waarheen?**	[vārheən?]
From where?	**Waarvandaan?**	[vārfandān?]
When?	**Wanneer?**	[vanneər?]
Why? (What for?)	**Hoekom?**	[hukom?]
Why? (~ are you crying?)	**Hoekom?**	[hukom?]

What for?	**Vir wat?**	[fir vat?]
How? (in what way)	**Hoe?**	[hu?]
What? (What kind of ...?)	**Watter?**	[vattər?]
Which?	**Watter een?**	[vattər eən?]

To whom?	**Vir wie?**	[fir vi?]
About whom?	**Oor wie?**	[oər vi?]
About what?	**Oor wat?**	[oər vat?]
With whom?	**Met wie?**	[met vi?]
How many? How much?	**Hoeveel?**	[hufeəl?]

4. Prepositions

with (accompanied by)	**met**	[met]
without	**sonder**	[sondər]
to (indicating direction)	**na**	[na]
about (talking ~ ...)	**oor**	[oər]
before (in time)	**voor**	[foər]
in front of ...	**voor ...**	[foər ...]
under (beneath, below)	**onder**	[ondər]

above (over)	oor	[oər]
on (atop)	op	[op]
from (off, out of)	uit	[œit]
of (made from)	van	[fan]

| in (e.g., ~ ten minutes) | oor | [oər] |
| over (across the top of) | oor | [oər] |

5. Function words. Adverbs. Part 1

Where? (at, in)	Waar?	[vār?]
here (adv)	hier	[hir]
there (adv)	daar	[dār]

| somewhere (to be) | êrens | [ærɛŋs] |
| nowhere (not anywhere) | nêrens | [nærɛŋs] |

| by (near, beside) | by | [baj] |
| by the window | by | [baj] |

Where (to)?	Waarheen?	[vārheən?]
here (e.g., come ~!)	hier	[hir]
there (e.g., to go ~)	soontoe	[soentu]
from here (adv)	hiervandaan	[hirfandān]
from there (adv)	daarvandaan	[dārfandān]

| close (adv) | naby | [nabaj] |
| far (adv) | ver | [fer] |

near (e.g., ~ Paris)	naby	[nabaj]
nearby (adv)	naby	[nabaj]
not far (adv)	nie ver nie	[ni fər ni]

left (adj)	linker-	[linkər-]
on the left	op linkerhand	[op linkərhant]
to the left	na links	[na links]

right (adj)	regter	[reχtər]
on the right	op regterhand	[op reχtərhant]
to the right	na regs	[na reχs]

in front (adv)	voor	[foər]
front (as adj)	voorste	[foərstə]
ahead (the kids ran ~)	vooruit	[foərœit]

behind (adv)	agter	[aχtər]
from behind	van agter	[fan aχtər]
back (towards the rear)	agtertoe	[aχtərtu]
middle	middel	[middəl]
in the middle	in die middel	[in di middəl]

at the side	op die sykant	[op di sajkant]
everywhere (adv)	orals	[orals]
around (in all directions)	orals rond	[orals ront]

from inside	van binne	[fan binnə]
somewhere (to go)	êrens	[ærɛŋs]
straight (directly)	reguit	[rexœit]
back (e.g., come ~)	terug	[teruχ]

| from anywhere | êrens vandaan | [ærɛŋs fandān] |
| from somewhere | êrens vandaan | [ærɛŋs fandān] |

firstly (adv)	in die eerste plek	[in di eərstə plek]
secondly (adv)	in die tweede plek	[in di tweədə plek]
thirdly (adv)	in die derde plek	[in di derdə plek]

suddenly (adv)	skielik	[skilik]
at first (in the beginning)	aan die begin	[ān di beχin]
for the first time	vir die eerste keer	[fir di eərstə keər]
long before …	lank voordat …	[lank foərdat …]
anew (over again)	opnuut	[opnɪt]
for good (adv)	vir goed	[fir χut]

never (adv)	nooit	[nojt]
again (adv)	weer	[veər]
now (adv)	nou	[næʊ]
often (adv)	dikwels	[dikwɛls]
then (adv)	toe	[tu]
urgently (quickly)	dringend	[driŋən]
usually (adv)	gewoonlik	[χevoənlik]

by the way, …	terloops, …	[terloəps], […]
possible (that is ~)	moontlik	[moentlik]
probably (adv)	waarskynlik	[vārskajnlik]
maybe (adv)	dalk	[dalk]
besides …	trouens...	[træʊɛŋs...]
that's why …	dis hoekom …	[dis hukom …]
in spite of …	ondanks …	[ondanks …]
thanks to …	danksy …	[danksaj …]

what (pron.)	wat	[vat]
that (conj.)	dat	[dat]
something	iets	[its]
anything (something)	iets	[its]
nothing	niks	[niks]

who (pron.)	wie	[vi]
someone	iemand	[imant]
somebody	iemand	[imant]

| nobody | niemand | [nimant] |
| nowhere (a voyage to ~) | nêrens | [nærɛŋs] |

| nobody's | niemand se | [nimant sə] |
| somebody's | iemand se | [imant sə] |

so (I'm ~ glad)	so	[so]
also (as well)	ook	[oək]
too (as well)	ook	[oək]

6. Function words. Adverbs. Part 2

Why?	Waarom?	[vārom?]
because ...	omdat ...	[omdat ...]
and	en	[ɛn]
or	of	[of]
but	maar	[mār]
for (e.g., ~ me)	vir	[fir]

too (~ many people)	te	[te]
only (exclusively)	net	[net]
exactly (adv)	presies	[presis]
about (more or less)	ongeveer	[onχəfeər]

approximately (adv)	ongeveer	[onχəfeər]
approximate (adj)	geraamde	[χerāmdə]
almost (adv)	amper	[ampər]
the rest	die res	[di res]

the other (second)	die ander	[di andər]
other (different)	ander	[andər]
each (adj)	elke	[ɛlkə]
any (no matter which)	enige	[ɛniχə]
many (adv)	baie	[baje]
much (adv)	baie	[baje]
many people	baie mense	[baje mɛŋsə]
all (everyone)	almal	[almal]

in return for ...	in ruil vir...	[in rœil fir...]
in exchange (adv)	as vergoeding	[as ferχudiŋ]
by hand (made)	met die hand	[met di hant]
hardly (negative opinion)	skaars	[skārs]

probably (adv)	waarskynlik	[vārskajnlik]
on purpose (intentionally)	opsetlik	[opsetlik]
by accident (adv)	toevallig	[tufalləχ]

very (adv)	baie	[baje]
for example (adv)	byvoorbeeld	[bajfoərbeəlt]
between	tussen	[tussən]
among	tussen	[tussən]
so much (such a lot)	so baie	[so baje]
especially (adv)	veral	[feral]

NUMBERS. MISCELLANEOUS

T&P Books Publishing

0 zero	**nul**	[nul]
1 one	**een**	[eən]
2 two	**twee**	[tweə]
3 three	**drie**	[dri]
4 four	**vier**	[fir]
5 five	**vyf**	[fajf]
6 six	**ses**	[ses]
7 seven	**sewe**	[sevə]
8 eight	**ag**	[aχ]
9 nine	**nege**	[neχə]
10 ten	**tien**	[tin]
11 eleven	**elf**	[ɛlf]
12 twelve	**twaalf**	[twālf]
13 thirteen	**dertien**	[dertin]
14 fourteen	**veertien**	[feərtin]
15 fifteen	**vyftien**	[fajftin]
16 sixteen	**sestien**	[sestin]
17 seventeen	**sewetien**	[sevətin]
18 eighteen	**agtien**	[aχtin]
19 nineteen	**negetien**	[neχetin]
20 twenty	**twintig**	[twintəχ]
21 twenty-one	**een-en-twintig**	[eən-en-twintəχ]
22 twenty-two	**twee-en-twintig**	[tweə-en-twintəχ]
23 twenty-three	**drie-en-twintig**	[dri-en-twintəχ]
30 thirty	**dertig**	[dertəχ]
31 thirty-one	**een-en-dertig**	[eən-en-dertəχ]
32 thirty-two	**twee-en-dertig**	[tweə-en-dertəχ]
33 thirty-three	**drie-en-dertig**	[dri-en-dertəχ]
40 forty	**veertig**	[feərtəχ]
41 forty-one	**een-en-veertig**	[eən-en-feərtəχ]
42 forty-two	**twee-en-veertig**	[tweə-en-feərtəχ]
43 forty-three	**vier-en-veertig**	[fir-en-feərtəχ]
50 fifty	**vyftig**	[fajftəχ]
51 fifty-one	**een-en-vyftig**	[eən-en-fajftəχ]
52 fifty-two	**twee-en-vyftig**	[tweə-en-fajftəχ]
53 fifty-three	**drie-en-vyftig**	[dri-en-fajftəχ]
60 sixty	**sestig**	[sestəχ]

61 sixty-one	**een-en-sestig**	[eən-en-sestəχ]
62 sixty-two	**twee-en-sestig**	[tweə-en-sestəχ]
63 sixty-three	**drie-en-sestig**	[dri-en-sestəχ]

70 seventy	**sewentig**	[seventəχ]
71 seventy-one	**een-en-sewentig**	[eən-en-seventəχ]
72 seventy-two	**twee-en-sewentig**	[tweə-en-seventəχ]
73 seventy-three	**drie-en-sewentig**	[dri-en-seventəχ]

80 eighty	**tagtig**	[taχtəχ]
81 eighty-one	**een-en-tagtig**	[eən-en-taχtəχ]
82 eighty-two	**twee-en-tagtig**	[tweə-en-taχtəχ]
83 eighty-three	**drie-en-tagtig**	[dri-en-taχtəχ]

90 ninety	**negentig**	[neχentəχ]
91 ninety-one	**een-en-negentig**	[eən-en-neχentəχ]
92 ninety-two	**twee-en-negentig**	[tweə-en-neχentəχ]
93 ninety-three	**drie-en-negentig**	[dri-en-neχentəχ]

8. Cardinal numbers. Part 2

100 one hundred	**honderd**	[hondərt]
200 two hundred	**tweehonderd**	[tweə·hondərt]
300 three hundred	**driehonderd**	[dri·hondərt]
400 four hundred	**vierhonderd**	[fir·hondərt]
500 five hundred	**vyfhonderd**	[fajf·hondərt]

600 six hundred	**seshonderd**	[ses·hondərt]
700 seven hundred	**sewehonderd**	[sevə·hondərt]
800 eight hundred	**aghonderd**	[aχ·hondərt]
900 nine hundred	**negehonderd**	[neχə·hondərt]

1000 one thousand	**duisend**	[dœisent]
2000 two thousand	**tweeduisend**	[tweə·dœisent]
3000 three thousand	**drieduisend**	[dri·dœisent]
10000 ten thousand	**tienduisend**	[tin·dœisent]
one hundred thousand	**honderdduisend**	[hondərt·dajsent]
million	**miljoen**	[miljun]
billion	**miljard**	[miljart]

9. Ordinal numbers

first (adj)	**eerste**	[eərstə]
second (adj)	**tweede**	[tweedə]
third (adj)	**derde**	[derdə]
fourth (adj)	**vierde**	[firdə]
fifth (adj)	**vyfde**	[fajfdə]
sixth (adj)	**sesde**	[sesdə]

seventh (adj)	**sewende**	[sevendə]
eighth (adj)	**agste**	[aχstə]
ninth (adj)	**negende**	[neχendə]
tenth (adj)	**tiende**	[tində]

COLOURS. UNITS OF MEASUREMENT

T&P Books Publishing

10. Colors

color	kleur	[kløər]
shade (tint)	skakering	[skakeriŋ]
hue	tint	[tint]
rainbow	reënboog	[reɛn·boəχ]

white (adj)	wit	[vit]
black (adj)	swart	[swart]
gray (adj)	grys	[χrajs]

green (adj)	groen	[χrun]
yellow (adj)	geel	[χeəl]
red (adj)	rooi	[roj]
blue (adj)	blou	[blæʊ]
light blue (adj)	ligblou	[liχ·blæʊ]
pink (adj)	pienk	[pink]
orange (adj)	oranje	[oranje]
violet (adj)	pers	[pers]
brown (adj)	bruin	[brœin]

golden (adj)	goue	[χæʊə]
silvery (adj)	silweragtig	[silweraχtəχ]
beige (adj)	beige	[bɛ:iʒ]
cream (adj)	roomkleurig	[roəm·kløərəχ]
turquoise (adj)	turkoois	[turkojs]
cherry red (adj)	kersierooi	[kersi·roj]
lilac (adj)	lila	[lila]
crimson (adj)	karmosyn	[karmosajn]

light (adj)	lig	[liχ]
dark (adj)	donker	[donkər]
bright, vivid (adj)	helder	[hɛldər]

colored (pencils)	kleurig	[kløərəχ]
color (e.g., ~ film)	kleur	[kløər]
black-and-white (adj)	swart-wit	[swart-wit]
plain (one-colored)	effe	[ɛffə]
multicolored (adj)	veelkleurig	[feəlkløərəχ]

11. Units of measurement

weight	gewig	[χevəχ]
length	lengte	[leŋtə]

width	breedte	[breədtə]
height	hoogte	[hoəχtə]
depth	diepte	[diptə]
volume	volume	[folumə]
area	area	[area]

gram	gram	[χram]
milligram	milligram	[milliχram]
kilogram	kilogram	[kiloχram]
ton	ton	[ton]
pound	pond	[pont]
ounce	ons	[ɔŋs]

meter	meter	[metər]
millimeter	millimeter	[millimetər]
centimeter	sentimeter	[sentimetər]
kilometer	kilometer	[kilometər]
mile	myl	[majl]

inch	duim	[dœim]
foot	voet	[fut]
yard	jaart	[jārt]

| square meter | vierkante meter | [firkantə metər] |
| hectare | hektaar | [hektār] |

liter	liter	[litər]
degree	graad	[χrāt]
volt	volt	[folt]
ampere	ampère	[ampɛːr]
horsepower	perdekrag	[perdə·kraχ]

quantity	hoeveelheid	[hufeəlhæjt]
half	helfte	[hɛlftə]
dozen	dosyn	[dosajn]
piece (item)	stuk	[stuk]

| size | grootte | [χroəttə] |
| scale (map ~) | skaal | [skāl] |

minimal (adj)	minimaal	[minimāl]
the smallest (adj)	die kleinste	[di klæjnstə]
medium (adj)	medium	[medium]
maximal (adj)	maksimaal	[maksimāl]
the largest (adj)	die grootste	[di χroətstə]

12. Containers

| canning jar (glass ~) | glaspot | [χlas·pot] |
| can | blikkie | [blikki] |

bucket	**emmer**	[ɛmmər]
barrel	**drom**	[drom]
wash basin (e.g., plastic ~)	**wasbak**	[vas·bak]
tank (100L water ~)	**tenk**	[tɛnk]
hip flask	**heupfles**	[høəp·fles]
jerrycan	**petrolblik**	[petrol·blik]
tank (e.g., tank car)	**tenk**	[tɛnk]
mug	**beker**	[bekər]
cup (of coffee, etc.)	**koppie**	[koppi]
saucer	**piering**	[piriŋ]
glass (tumbler)	**glas**	[χlas]
wine glass	**wynglas**	[vajn·χlas]
stock pot (soup pot)	**soppot**	[sop·pot]
bottle (~ of wine)	**bottel**	[bottəl]
neck (of the bottle, etc.)	**nek**	[nek]
carafe (decanter)	**kraffie**	[kraffi]
pitcher	**kruik**	[krœik]
vessel (container)	**houer**	[hæʋər]
pot (crock, stoneware ~)	**pot**	[pot]
vase	**vaas**	[fãs]
bottle (perfume ~)	**bottel**	[bottəl]
vial, small bottle	**botteltjie**	[bottɛlki]
tube (of toothpaste)	**buisie**	[bœisi]
sack (bag)	**sak**	[sak]
bag (paper ~, plastic ~)	**sak**	[sak]
pack (of cigarettes, etc.)	**pakkie**	[pakki]
box (e.g., shoebox)	**kartondoos**	[karton·doəs]
crate	**krat**	[krat]
basket	**mandjie**	[mandʒi]

MAIN VERBS

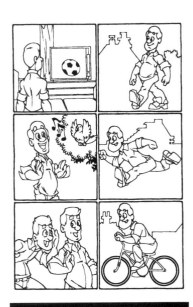

T&P Books Publishing

to advise (vt)	**aanraai**	[ānrāi]
to agree (say yes)	**saamstem**	[sāmstem]
to answer (vi, vt)	**antwoord**	[antwoərt]
to apologize (vi)	**verskoning vra**	[ferskoniŋ fra]
to arrive (vi)	**aankom**	[ānkom]
to ask (~ oneself)	**vra**	[fra]
to ask (~ sb to do sth)	**vra**	[fra]
to be (vi)	**wees**	[veəs]
to be afraid	**bang wees**	[baŋ veəs]
to be hungry	**honger wees**	[hoŋər veəs]
to be interested in ...	**belangstel in ...**	[belaŋstəl in ...]
to be needed	**nodig wees**	[nodəχ veəs]
to be surprised	**verbaas wees**	[ferbās veəs]
to be thirsty	**dors wees**	[dors veəs]
to begin (vt)	**begin**	[beχin]
to belong to ...	**behoort aan ...**	[behoərt ān ...]
to boast (vi)	**spog**	[spoχ]
to break (split into pieces)	**breek**	[breək]
to call (~ for help)	**roep**	[rup]
can (v aux)	**kan**	[kan]
to catch (vt)	**vang**	[faŋ]
to change (vt)	**verander**	[ferandər]
to choose (select)	**kies**	[kis]
to come down (the stairs)	**afkom**	[afkom]
to compare (vt)	**vergelyk**	[ferχəlajk]
to complain (vi, vt)	**kla**	[kla]
to confuse (mix up)	**verwar**	[ferwar]
to continue (vt)	**aangaan**	[ānχān]
to control (vt)	**kontroleer**	[kontroleər]
to cook (dinner)	**kook**	[koək]
to cost (vt)	**kos**	[kos]
to count (add up)	**tel**	[təl]
to count on ...	**reken op ...**	[reken op ...]
to create (vt)	**skep**	[skep]
to cry (weep)	**huil**	[hœil]

14. The most important verbs. Part 2

to deceive (vi, vt)	bedrieg	[bedrəχ]
to decorate (tree, street)	versier	[fersir]
to defend (a country, etc.)	verdedig	[ferdedəχ]
to demand (request firmly)	eis	[æjs]
to dig (vt)	grawe	[χravə]
to discuss (vt)	bespreek	[bespreək]
to do (vt)	doen	[dun]
to doubt (have doubts)	twyfel	[twajfəl]
to drop (let fall)	laat val	[lāt fal]
to enter (room, house, etc.)	binnegaan	[binnəχān]
to excuse (forgive)	verskoon	[ferskoən]
to exist (vi)	bestaan	[bestān]
to expect (foresee)	voorsien	[foərsin]
to explain (vt)	verduidelik	[ferdœidəlik]
to fall (vi)	val	[fal]
to find (vt)	vind	[fint]
to finish (vt)	klaarmaak	[klārmāk]
to fly (vi)	vlieg	[fliχ]
to follow ... (come after)	volg ...	[folχ ...]
to forget (vi, vt)	vergeet	[ferχeət]
to forgive (vt)	vergewe	[ferχevə]
to give (vt)	gee	[χeə]
to go (on foot)	gaan	[χān]
to go for a swim	gaan swem	[χān swem]
to go out (for dinner, etc.)	uitgaan	[œitχān]
to guess (the answer)	raai	[rāi]
to have (vt)	hê	[hɛ:]
to have breakfast	ontbyt	[ontbajt]
to have dinner	aandete gebruik	[āndetə χebrœik]
to have lunch	gaan eet	[χān eət]
to hear (vt)	hoor	[hoər]
to help (vt)	help	[hɛlp]
to hide (vt)	wegsteek	[veχsteək]
to hope (vi, vt)	hoop	[hoəp]
to hunt (vi, vt)	jag	[jaχ]
to hurry (vi)	opskud	[opskut]

15. The most important verbs. Part 3

to inform (vt)	in kennis stel	[in kɛnnis stəl]
to insist (vi, vt)	aandring	[āndriŋ]

to insult (vt)	beledig	[beledəχ]
to invite (vt)	uitnooi	[œitnoj]
to joke (vi)	grappies maak	[χrappis māk]

to keep (vt)	bewaar	[bevār]
to keep silent	stilbly	[stilblaj]
to kill (vt)	doodmaak	[doədmāk]
to know (sb)	ken	[ken]
to know (sth)	weet	[veət]
to laugh (vi)	lag	[laχ]

to liberate (city, etc.)	bevry	[befraj]
to like (I like …)	hou van	[hæʊ fan]
to look for … (search)	soek …	[suk …]
to love (sb)	liefhê	[lifhɛ:]

to manage, to run	beheer	[beheər]
to mean (signify)	beteken	[betekən]
to mention (talk about)	verwys na	[ferwajs na]
to miss (school, etc.)	bank	[bank]
to notice (see)	raaksien	[rāksin]

to object (vi, vt)	beswaar maak	[beswār māk]
to observe (see)	waarneem	[vārneəm]
to open (vt)	oopmaak	[oəpmāk]
to order (meal, etc.)	bestel	[bestəl]
to order (mil.)	beveel	[befeəl]
to own (possess)	besit	[besit]

to participate (vi)	deelneem	[deəlneəm]
to pay (vi, vt)	betaal	[betāl]
to permit (vt)	toestaan	[tustān]
to plan (vt)	beplan	[beplan]
to play (children)	speel	[speəl]

to pray (vi, vt)	bid	[bit]
to prefer (vt)	verkies	[ferkis]
to promise (vt)	beloof	[beloəf]
to pronounce (vt)	uitspreek	[œitspreək]
to propose (vt)	voorstel	[foərstəl]
to punish (vt)	straf	[straf]

16. The most important verbs. Part 4

to read (vi, vt)	lees	[leəs]
to recommend (vt)	aanbeveel	[ānbefeəl]
to refuse (vi, vt)	weier	[væjer]
to regret (be sorry)	jammer wees	[jammər veəs]
to rent (sth from sb)	huur	[hɪr]
to repeat (say again)	herhaal	[herhāl]

to reserve, to book	**bespreek**	[bespreek]
to run (vi)	**hardloop**	[hardloəp]
to save (rescue)	**red**	[ret]
to say (~ thank you)	**sê**	[sɛ:]
to scold (vt)	**uitvaar teen**	[œitfãr teən]
to see (vt)	**sien**	[sin]
to sell (vt)	**verkoop**	[ferkoəp]
to send (vt)	**stuur**	[stɪr]
to shoot (vi)	**skiet**	[skit]
to shout (vi)	**skreeu**	[skriʊ]
to show (vt)	**wys**	[vajs]
to sign (document)	**teken**	[tekən]
to sit down (vi)	**gaan sit**	[χãn sit]
to smile (vi)	**glimlag**	[χlimlaχ]
to speak (vi, vt)	**praat**	[prãt]
to steal (money, etc.)	**steel**	[steəl]
to stop (for pause, etc.)	**stilhou**	[stilhæʊ]
to stop	**ophou**	[ophæʊ]
(please ~ calling me)		
to study (vt)	**studeer**	[studeər]
to swim (vi)	**swem**	[swem]
to take (vt)	**vat**	[fat]
to think (vi, vt)	**dink**	[dink]
to threaten (vt)	**dreig**	[dræjχ]
to touch (with hands)	**aanraak**	[ãnrãk]
to translate (vt)	**vertaal**	[fertãl]
to trust (vt)	**vertrou**	[fertræʊ]
to try (attempt)	**probeer**	[probeər]
to turn (e.g., ~ left)	**draai**	[drãi]
to underestimate (vt)	**onderskat**	[ondərskat]
to understand (vt)	**verstaan**	[ferstãn]
to unite (vt)	**verenig**	[ferenəχ]
to wait (vt)	**wag**	[vaχ]
to want (wish, desire)	**wil**	[vil]
to warn (vt)	**waarsku**	[vãrsku]
to work (vi)	**werk**	[verk]
to write (vt)	**skryf**	[skrajf]
to write down	**opskryf**	[opskrajf]

TIME. CALENDAR

T&P Books Publishing

17. Weekdays

Monday	**Maandag**	[māndaχ]
Tuesday	**Dinsdag**	[dinsdaχ]
Wednesday	**Woensdag**	[voɛŋsdaχ]
Thursday	**Donderdag**	[dondərdaχ]
Friday	**Vrydag**	[frajdaχ]
Saturday	**Saterdag**	[satərdaχ]
Sunday	**Sondag**	[sondaχ]

today (adv)	**vandag**	[fandaχ]
tomorrow (adv)	**môre**	[mɔrə]
the day after tomorrow	**oormôre**	[oərmɔrə]
yesterday (adv)	**gister**	[χistər]
the day before yesterday	**eergister**	[eərχistər]

day	**dag**	[daχ]
working day	**werksdag**	[verks·daχ]
public holiday	**openbare vakansiedag**	[openbarə fakaŋsi·daχ]
day off	**verlofdag**	[ferlofdaχ]
weekend	**naweek**	[naveək]

all day long	**die hele dag**	[di helə daχ]
the next day (adv)	**die volgende dag**	[di folχendə daχ]
two days ago	**twee dae gelede**	[tweə daə χeledə]
the day before	**die dag voor**	[di daχ foər]
daily (adj)	**daeliks**	[daəliks]
every day (adv)	**elke dag**	[ɛlkə daχ]

week	**week**	[veək]
last week (adv)	**laas week**	[lās veək]
next week (adv)	**volgende week**	[folχendə veək]
weekly (adj)	**weekliks**	[veəkliks]
every week (adv)	**weekliks**	[veəkliks]
every Tuesday	**elke Dinsdag**	[ɛlkə dinsdaχ]

18. Hours. Day and night

morning	**oggend**	[oχent]
in the morning	**soggens**	[soχɛŋs]
noon, midday	**middag**	[middaχ]
in the afternoon	**in die namiddag**	[in di namiddaχ]
evening	**aand**	[ānt]
in the evening	**saans**	[sāŋs]

night	nag	[naχ]
at night	snags	[snaχs]
midnight	middernag	[middərnaχ]
second	sekonde	[sekondə]
minute	minuut	[minɪt]
hour	uur	[ɪr]
half an hour	n halfuur	[n halfɪr]
fifteen minutes	vyftien minute	[fajftin minutə]
24 hours	24 ure	[fir-en-twintəχ urə]
sunrise	sonop	[son·op]
dawn	daeraad	[daerãt]
early morning	elke oggend	[ɛlkə oχent]
sunset	sononder	[son·ondər]
early in the morning	vroegdag	[fruχdaχ]
this morning	vanmôre	[fanmɔrə]
tomorrow morning	môreoggend	[mɔrə·oχent]
this afternoon	vanmiddag	[fanmiddaχ]
in the afternoon	in die namiddag	[in di namiddaχ]
tomorrow afternoon	môremiddag	[mɔrə·middaχ]
tonight (this evening)	vanaand	[fanãnt]
tomorrow night	môreaand	[mɔrə·ãnt]
at 3 o'clock sharp	klokslag 3 uur	[klokslaχ dri ɪr]
about 4 o'clock	omstreeks 4 uur	[omstreeks fir ɪr]
by 12 o'clock	teen 12 uur	[teən twalf ɪr]
in 20 minutes	oor twintig minute	[oər twintəχ minutə]
on time (adv)	betyds	[betajds]
a quarter of ...	kwart voor ...	[kwart foər ...]
every 15 minutes	elke 15 minute	[ɛlkə fajftin minutə]
round the clock	24 uur per dag	[fir-en-twintəχ pər daχ]

19. Months. Seasons

January	Januarie	[januari]
February	Februarie	[februari]
March	Maart	[mãrt]
April	April	[april]
May	Mei	[mæj]
June	Junie	[juni]
July	Julie	[juli]
August	Augustus	[ɔuχustus]
September	September	[septembər]

October	**Oktober**	[oktobər]
November	**November**	[nofembər]
December	**Desember**	[desembər]

spring	**lente**	[lentə]
in spring	**in die lente**	[in di lentə]
spring (as adj)	**lente-**	[lente-]

summer	**somer**	[somər]
in summer	**in die somer**	[in di somər]
summer (as adj)	**somerse**	[somersə]

fall	**herfs**	[herfs]
in fall	**in die herfs**	[in di herfs]
fall (as adj)	**herfsagtige**	[herfsaχtiχə]

winter	**winter**	[vintər]
in winter	**in die winter**	[in di vintər]
winter (as adj)	**winter-**	[vintər-]

month	**maand**	[mānt]
this month	**hierdie maand**	[hirdi mānt]
next month	**volgende maand**	[folχendə mānt]
last month	**laasmaand**	[lāsmānt]
in 2 months (2 months later)	**oor twe maande**	[oər twe māndə]
the whole month	**die hele maand**	[di helə mānt]

monthly (~ magazine)	**maandeliks**	[māndəliks]
monthly (adv)	**maandeliks**	[māndəliks]
every month	**elke maand**	[ɛlkə mānt]

year	**jaar**	[jār]
this year	**hierdie jaar**	[hirdi jār]
next year	**volgende jaar**	[folχendə jār]
last year	**laasjaar**	[lāʃār]

| in two years | **binne twee jaar** | [binnə tweə jār] |
| the whole year | **die hele jaar** | [di helə jār] |

every year	**elke jaar**	[ɛlkə jār]
annual (adj)	**jaarliks**	[jārliks]
annually (adv)	**jaarliks**	[jārliks]
4 times a year	**4 keer per jaar**	[fir keər pər jār]

date (e.g., today's ~)	**datum**	[datum]
date (e.g., ~ of birth)	**datum**	[datum]
calendar	**kalender**	[kalendər]

six months	**ses maande**	[ses māndə]
season (summer, etc.)	**seisoen**	[sæjsun]
century	**eeu**	[iʊ]

TRAVEL. HOTEL

USD CAD
EUR CHF
JPY HKD
GBP CNY

RECEPTION

T&P Books Publishing

20. Trip. Travel

tourism, travel	**toerisme**	[turismə]
tourist	**toeris**	[turis]
trip, voyage	**reis**	[ræjs]
adventure	**avontuur**	[afontɹr]
trip, journey	**reis**	[ræjs]
vacation	**vakansie**	[fakaŋsi]
to be on vacation	**met vakansie wees**	[met fakaŋsi veəs]
rest	**rus**	[rus]
train	**trein**	[træjn]
by train	**per trein**	[pər træjn]
airplane	**vliegtuig**	[fliχtœiχ]
by airplane	**per vliegtuig**	[pər fliχtœiχ]
by car	**per motor**	[pər motor]
by ship	**per skip**	[pər skip]
luggage	**bagasie**	[baχasi]
suitcase	**tas**	[tas]
luggage cart	**bagasiekarretjie**	[baχasi·karrəki]
passport	**paspoort**	[paspoərt]
visa	**visum**	[fisum]
ticket	**kaartjie**	[kārki]
air ticket	**lugkaartjie**	[luχ·kārki]
guidebook	**reisgids**	[ræjsχids]
map (tourist ~)	**kaart**	[kārt]
area (rural ~)	**gebied**	[χebit]
place, site	**plek**	[plek]
exotica (n)	**eksotiese dinge**	[ɛksotisə diŋə]
exotic (adj)	**eksoties**	[ɛksotis]
amazing (adj)	**verbasend**	[ferbasent]
group	**groep**	[χrup]
excursion, sightseeing tour	**uitstappie**	[œitstappi]
guide (person)	**gids**	[χids]

21. Hotel

hotel	**hotel**	[hotəl]
motel	**motel**	[motəl]

three-star (~ hotel)	**drie-ster**	[dri-stər]
five-star	**vyf-ster**	[fajf-stər]
to stay (in a hotel, etc.)	**oornag**	[oərnaχ]
room	**kamer**	[kamər]
single room	**enkelkamer**	[ɛnkəl·kamər]
double room	**dubbelkamer**	[dubbəl·kamər]
half board	**met aandete,**	[met āndetə],
	bed en ontbyt	[bet en ontbajt]
full board	**volle losies**	[follə losis]
with bath	**met bad**	[met bat]
with shower	**met stortbad**	[met stort·bat]
satellite television	**satelliet-TV**	[satɛllit-te·fe]
air-conditioner	**lugversorger**	[luχfersorχər]
towel	**handdoek**	[handduk]
key	**sleutel**	[sløətəl]
administrator	**bestuurder**	[bestɪrdər]
chambermaid	**kamermeisie**	[kamər·mæjsi]
porter, bellboy	**hoteljoggie**	[hotəl·joχi]
doorman	**portier**	[portir]
restaurant	**restaurant**	[restɔurant]
pub, bar	**kroeg**	[kruχ]
breakfast	**ontbyt**	[ontbajt]
dinner	**aandete**	[āndetə]
buffet	**buffetete**	[buffetetə]
lobby	**voorportaal**	[foər·portāl]
elevator	**hysbak**	[hajsbak]
DO NOT DISTURB	**MOENIE STEUR NIE**	[muni støər ni]
NO SMOKING	**ROOK VERBODE**	[roək ferbodə]

22. Sightseeing

monument	**monument**	[monument]
fortress	**fort**	[fort]
palace	**paleis**	[palæjs]
castle	**kasteel**	[kasteəl]
tower	**toring**	[toriŋ]
mausoleum	**mausoleum**	[mɔusoløəm]
architecture	**argitektuur**	[arχitektɪr]
medieval (adj)	**Middeleeus**	[middeliʋs]
ancient (adj)	**oud**	[æʋt]
national (adj)	**nasionaal**	[naʃionāl]
famous (monument, etc.)	**bekend**	[bekent]

tourist	**toeris**	[turis]
guide (person)	**gids**	[χids]
excursion, sightseeing tour	**uitstappie**	[œitstappi]
to show (vt)	**wys**	[vajs]
to tell (vt)	**vertel**	[fertəl]
to find (vt)	**vind**	[fint]
to get lost (lose one's way)	**verdwaal**	[ferdwāl]
map (e.g., subway ~)	**kaart**	[kārt]
map (e.g., city ~)	**kaart**	[kārt]
souvenir, gift	**aandenking**	[āndenkiŋ]
gift shop	**geskenkwinkel**	[χeskɛnk·vinkəl]
to take pictures	**fotografeer**	[fotoχrafeər]
to have one's picture taken	**jou portret laat maak**	[jæʋ portret lāt māk]

TRANSPORTATION

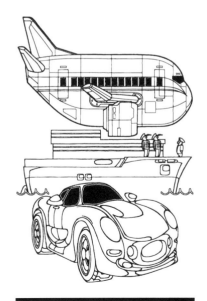

T&P Books Publishing

23. Airport

airport	**lughawe**	[luχhavə]
airplane	**vliegtuig**	[fliχtœiχ]
airline	**lugredery**	[luχrederaj]
air traffic controller	**lugverkeersleier**	[luχ·ferkeərs·læjer]
departure	**vertrek**	[fertrek]
arrival	**aankoms**	[ānkoms]
to arrive (by plane)	**aankom**	[ānkom]
departure time	**vertrektyd**	[fertrək·tajt]
arrival time	**aankomstyd**	[ānkoms·tajt]
to be delayed	**vertraag wees**	[fertrāχ veəs]
flight delay	**vlugvertraging**	[fluχ·fertraχiŋ]
information board	**informasiebord**	[informasi·bort]
information	**informasie**	[informasi]
to announce (vt)	**aankondig**	[ānkondəχ]
flight (e.g., next ~)	**vlug**	[fluχ]
customs	**doeane**	[duanə]
customs officer	**doeanebeampte**	[duanə·beamptə]
customs declaration	**doeaneverklaring**	[duanə·ferklariŋ]
to fill out (vt)	**invul**	[inful]
passport control	**paspoortkontrole**	[paspoərt·kontrolə]
luggage	**bagasie**	[baχasi]
hand luggage	**handbagasie**	[hand·baχasi]
luggage cart	**bagasiekarretjie**	[baχasi·karrəki]
landing	**landing**	[landiŋ]
landing strip	**landingsbaan**	[landiŋs·bān]
to land (vi)	**land**	[lant]
airstairs	**vliegtuigtrap**	[fliχtœiχ·trap]
check-in	**na die vertrektoonbank**	[na di fertrək·toənbank]
check-in counter	**vertrektoonbank**	[fertrək·toənbank]
to check-in (vi)	**na die vertrektoonbank gaan**	[na di fertrək·toənbank χān]
boarding pass	**instapkaart**	[instap·kārt]
departure gate	**vertrekuitgang**	[fertrek·œitχaŋ]
transit	**transito**	[traŋsito]
to wait (vt)	**wag**	[vaχ]

departure lounge	vertreksaal	[fertrək·sāl]
to see off	afsien	[afsin]
to say goodbye	afskeid neem	[afskæjt neəm]

24. Airplane

airplane	vliegtuig	[fliχtœiχ]
air ticket	lugkaartjie	[luχ·kārki]
airline	lugredery	[luχrederəj]
airport	lughawe	[luχhavə]
supersonic (adj)	supersonies	[supersonis]

captain	kaptein	[kaptæjn]
crew	bemanning	[bemanniŋ]
pilot	piloot	[piloət]
flight attendant (fem.)	lugwaardin	[luχ·wārdin]
navigator	navigator	[nafiχator]

wings	vlerke	[flerkə]
tail	stert	[stert]
cockpit	stuurkajuit	[stɪr·kajœit]
engine	enjin	[ɛndʒin]
undercarriage (landing gear)	landingstel	[landiŋ·stəl]
turbine	turbine	[turbinə]

propeller	skroef	[skruf]
black box	swart boks	[swart boks]
yoke (control column)	stuurstang	[stɪr·staŋ]
fuel	brandstof	[brantstof]
safety card	veiligheidskaart	[fæjliχæjts·kārt]
oxygen mask	suurstofmasker	[sɪrstof·maskər]
uniform	uniform	[uniform]
life vest	reddingsbaadjie	[rɛddiŋs·bādʒi]
parachute	valskerm	[fal·skerm]

takeoff	opstyging	[opstajχiŋ]
to take off (vi)	opstyg	[opstajχ]
runway	landingsbaan	[landiŋs·bān]

visibility	uitsig	[œitsəχ]
flight (act of flying)	vlug	[fluχ]
altitude	hoogte	[hoəχtə]
air pocket	lugsak	[luχsak]

seat	sitplek	[sitplek]
headphones	koptelefoon	[kop·telefoən]
folding tray (tray table)	voutafeltjie	[fæu·tafɛlki]
airplane window	vliegtuigvenster	[fliχtœiχ·fɛŋstər]
aisle	paadjie	[pādʒi]

25. Train

train	trein	[træjn]
commuter train	voorstedelike trein	[foərstedelikə træjn]
express train	sneltrein	[snɛl·træjn]
diesel locomotive	diesellokomotief	[disəl·lokomotif]
steam locomotive	stoomlokomotief	[stoəm·lokomotif]
passenger car	passasierswa	[passasirs·wa]
dining car	eetwa	[eət·wa]
rails	spoorstawe	[spoər·stavə]
railroad	spoorweg	[spoər·weχ]
railway tie	dwarslêer	[dwarslɛar]
platform (railway ~)	perron	[perron]
track (~ 1, 2, etc.)	spoor	[spoər]
semaphore	semafoor	[semafoər]
station	stasie	[stasi]
engineer (train driver)	treindrywer	[træjn·drajvər]
porter (of luggage)	portier	[portir]
car attendant	kondukteur	[konduktøər]
passenger	passasier	[passasir]
conductor (ticket inspector)	kondukteur	[konduktøər]
corridor (in train)	gang	[χaŋ]
emergency brake	noodrem	[noədrem]
compartment	kompartiment	[kompartiment]
berth	bed	[bet]
upper berth	boonste bed	[boəŋstə bet]
lower berth	onderste bed	[ondərstə bet]
bed linen, bedding	beddegoed	[beddə·χut]
ticket	kaartjie	[kārki]
schedule	diensrooster	[diŋs·roəstər]
information display	informasiebord	[informasi·bort]
to leave, to depart	vertrek	[fertrek]
departure (of train)	vertrek	[fertrek]
to arrive (ab. train)	aankom	[ānkom]
arrival	aankoms	[ānkoms]
to arrive by train	aankom per trein	[ānkom pər træjn]
to get on the train	in die trein klim	[in di træjn klim]
to get off the train	uit die trein klim	[œit di træjn klim]
train wreck	treinbotsing	[træjn·botsiŋ]
to derail (vi)	ontspoor	[ontspoər]

steam locomotive	**stoomlokomotief**	[stoəm·lokomotif]
stoker, fireman	**stoker**	[stokər]
firebox	**stookplek**	[stoəkplek]
coal	**steenkool**	[steən·koəl]

26. Ship

ship	**skip**	[skip]
vessel	**vaartuig**	[fārtœiχ]
steamship	**stoomboot**	[stoəm·boət]
riverboat	**rivierboot**	[rifir·boət]
cruise ship	**toerskip**	[tur·skip]
cruiser	**kruiser**	[krœisər]
yacht	**jag**	[jaχ]
tugboat	**sleepboot**	[sleəp·boət]
barge	**vragskuit**	[fraχ·skœit]
ferry	**veerboot**	[feər·boət]
sailing ship	**seilskip**	[sæjl·skip]
brigantine	**skoenerbrik**	[skunər·brik]
ice breaker	**ysbreker**	[ajs·brekər]
submarine	**duikboot**	[dœik·boət]
boat (flat-bottomed ~)	**roeiboot**	[ruiboət]
dinghy	**bootjie**	[boəki]
lifeboat	**reddingsboot**	[rɛddiŋs·boət]
motorboat	**motorboot**	[motor·boət]
captain	**kaptein**	[kaptæjn]
seaman	**seeman**	[seəman]
sailor	**matroos**	[matroəs]
crew	**bemanning**	[bemanniŋ]
boatswain	**bootsman**	[boətsman]
ship's boy	**skeepsjonge**	[skeəps·joŋə]
cook	**kok**	[kok]
ship's doctor	**skeepsdokter**	[skeəps·doktər]
deck	**dek**	[dek]
mast	**mas**	[mas]
sail	**seil**	[sæjl]
hold	**skeepsruim**	[skeəps·rœim]
bow (prow)	**boeg**	[buχ]
stern	**agterstewe**	[aχtərstevə]
oar	**roeispaan**	[ruis·pān]
screw propeller	**skroef**	[skruf]

cabin	kajuit	[kajœit]
wardroom	offisierskajuit	[offisirs·kajœit]
engine room	enjinkamer	[ɛndʒin·kamər]
bridge	brug	[bruχ]
radio room	radiokamer	[radio·kamər]
wave (radio)	golf	[χolf]
logbook	logboek	[loχbuk]

spyglass	verkyker	[ferkajkər]
bell	bel	[bəl]
flag	vlag	[flaχ]

| hawser (mooring ~) | kabel | [kabəl] |
| knot (bowline, etc.) | knoop | [knoəp] |

| deckrails | dekleuning | [dek·løəniŋ] |
| gangway | gangplank | [χaŋ·plank] |

anchor	anker	[ankər]
to weigh anchor	anker lig	[ankər ləχ]
to drop anchor	anker uitgooi	[ankər œitχoj]
anchor chain	ankerketting	[ankər·kɛttiŋ]

port (harbor)	hawe	[havə]
quay, wharf	kaai	[kāi]
to berth (moor)	vasmeer	[fasmeər]
to cast off	vertrek	[fertrek]

trip, voyage	reis	[ræjs]
cruise (sea trip)	cruise	[kru:s]
course (route)	koers	[kurs]
route (itinerary)	roete	[rutə]

fairway (safe water channel)	vaarwater	[fār·vatər]
shallows	sandbank	[sand·bank]
to run aground	strand	[strant]

storm	storm	[storm]
signal	sienjaal	[sinjāl]
to sink (vi)	sink	[sink]
Man overboard!	Man oorboord!	[man oərboərd!]
SOS (distress signal)	SOS	[sos]
ring buoy	reddingsboei	[rɛddiŋs·bui]

CITY

T&P Books Publishing

bus	**bus**	[bus]
streetcar	**trem**	[trem]
trolley bus	**trembus**	[trembus]
route (of bus, etc.)	**busroete**	[bus·rutə]
number (e.g., bus ~)	**nommer**	[nommər]
to go by ...	**ry per ...**	[raj pər ...]
to get on (~ the bus)	**inklim**	[inklim]
to get off ...	**uitklim ...**	[œitklim ...]
stop (e.g., bus ~)	**halte**	[haltə]
next stop	**volgende halte**	[folχendə haltə]
terminus	**eindpunt**	[æjnd·punt]
schedule	**diensrooster**	[diŋs·roəstər]
to wait (vt)	**wag**	[vaχ]
ticket	**kaartjie**	[kārki]
fare	**reistarief**	[ræjs·tarif]
cashier (ticket seller)	**kaartjieverkoper**	[kārki·ferkopər]
ticket inspection	**kaartjiekontrole**	[kārki·kontrolə]
ticket inspector	**kontroleur**	[kontroløər]
to be late (for ...)	**laat wees**	[lāt veəs]
to miss (~ the train, etc.)	**mis**	[mis]
to be in a hurry	**haastig wees**	[hāstəχ veəs]
taxi, cab	**taxi**	[taksi]
taxi driver	**taxibestuurder**	[taksi·bestɪrdər]
by taxi	**per taxi**	[pər taksi]
taxi stand	**taxistaanplek**	[taksi·stānplek]
traffic	**verkeer**	[ferkeər]
traffic jam	**verkeersknoop**	[ferkeərs·knoəp]
rush hour	**spitsuur**	[spits·ɪr]
to park (vi)	**parkeer**	[parkeər]
to park (vt)	**parkeer**	[parkeər]
parking lot	**parkeerterrein**	[parkeər·terræjn]
subway	**metro**	[metro]
station	**stasie**	[stasi]
to take the subway	**die metro vat**	[di metro fat]
train	**trein**	[træjn]
train station	**treinstasie**	[træjn·stasi]

28. City. Life in the city

city, town	**stad**	[stat]
capital city	**hoofstad**	[hoəf·stat]
village	**dorp**	[dorp]
city map	**stadskaart**	[stats·kārt]
downtown	**sentrum**	[sentrum]
suburb	**voorstad**	[foərstat]
suburban (adj)	**voorstedelik**	[foərstedelik]
outskirts	**buitewyke**	[bœitəvajkə]
environs (suburbs)	**omgewing**	[omχeviŋ]
city block	**stadswyk**	[stats·wajk]
residential block (area)	**woonbuurt**	[voənbɪrt]
traffic	**verkeer**	[ferkeər]
traffic lights	**robot**	[robot]
public transportation	**openbare vervoer**	[openbarə ferfur]
intersection	**kruispunt**	[krœis·punt]
crosswalk	**sebraoorgang**	[sebra·oərχaŋ]
pedestrian underpass	**voetgangertonnel**	[futχaŋər·tonnəl]
to cross (~ the street)	**oorsteek**	[oərsteək]
pedestrian	**voetganger**	[futχaŋər]
sidewalk	**sypaadjie**	[saj·pādʒi]
bridge	**brug**	[bruχ]
embankment (river walk)	**wal**	[val]
fountain	**fontein**	[fontæjn]
allée (garden walkway)	**laning**	[laniŋ]
park	**park**	[park]
boulevard	**boulevard**	[bulefar]
square	**plein**	[plæjn]
avenue (wide street)	**laan**	[lān]
street	**straat**	[strāt]
side street	**systraat**	[saj·strāt]
dead end	**doodloopstraat**	[doədloəp·strāt]
house	**huis**	[hœis]
building	**gebou**	[χebæʊ]
skyscraper	**wolkekrabber**	[volkə·krabbər]
facade	**gewel**	[χevəl]
roof	**dak**	[dak]
window	**venster**	[fɛŋstər]
arch	**arkade**	[arkadə]
column	**kolom**	[kolom]
corner	**hoek**	[huk]
store window	**uitstalraam**	[œitstalrām]

signboard (store sign, etc.)	**reklamebord**	[reklamə·bort]
poster	**plakkaat**	[plakkāt]
advertising poster	**reklameplakkaat**	[reklamə·plakkāt]
billboard	**aanplakbord**	[ānplakbort]
garbage, trash	**vullis**	[fullis]
trashcan (public ~)	**vullisbak**	[fullis·bak]
to litter (vi)	**rommel strooi**	[romməl stroj]
garbage dump	**vullishoop**	[fullis·hoəp]
phone booth	**telefoonhokkie**	[telefoən·hokki]
lamppost	**lamppaal**	[lamp·pāl]
bench (park ~)	**bank**	[bank]
police officer	**polisieman**	[polisi·man]
police	**polisie**	[polisi]
beggar	**bedelaar**	[bedelār]
homeless (n)	**daklose**	[daklosə]

29. Urban institutions

store	**winkel**	[vinkəl]
drugstore, pharmacy	**apteek**	[apteək]
eyeglass store	**optisiên**	[optisiɛn]
shopping mall	**winkelsentrum**	[vinkəl·sentrum]
supermarket	**supermark**	[supermark]
bakery	**bakkery**	[bakkeraj]
baker	**bakker**	[bakkər]
pastry shop	**banketbakkery**	[banket·bakkeraj]
grocery store	**kruidenierswinkel**	[krœidenirs·vinkəl]
butcher shop	**slagter**	[slaχtər]
produce store	**groentewinkel**	[χruntə·vinkəl]
market	**mark**	[mark]
coffee house	**koffiekroeg**	[koffi·kruχ]
restaurant	**restaurant**	[restɔurant]
pub, bar	**kroeg**	[kruχ]
pizzeria	**pizzeria**	[pizzeria]
hair salon	**haarsalon**	[hār·salon]
post office	**poskantoor**	[pos·kantoər]
dry cleaners	**droogskoonmakers**	[droəχ·skoən·makers]
photo studio	**fotostudio**	[foto·studio]
shoe store	**skoenwinkel**	[skun·vinkəl]
bookstore	**boekhandel**	[buk·handəl]
sporting goods store	**sportwinkel**	[sport·vinkəl]
clothes repair shop	**klereherstelwinkel**	[klerə·herstəl·vinkəl]

formal wear rental	**klereverhuurwinkel**	[klerə·ferhɪr·vinkəl]
video rental store	**videowinkel**	[video·vinkəl]
circus	**sirkus**	[sirkus]
zoo	**dieretuin**	[dirə·tœin]
movie theater	**bioskoop**	[bioskoəp]
museum	**museum**	[musøəm]
library	**biblioteek**	[biblioteək]
theater	**teater**	[teatər]
opera (opera house)	**opera**	[opera]
nightclub	**nagklub**	[naχ·klup]
casino	**kasino**	[kasino]
mosque	**moskee**	[moskeə]
synagogue	**sinagoge**	[sinaχoχə]
cathedral	**katedraal**	[katedrāl]
temple	**tempel**	[tempəl]
church	**kerk**	[kerk]
college	**kollege**	[kolledʒ]
university	**universiteit**	[unifersitæjt]
school	**skool**	[skoəl]
prefecture	**stadhuis**	[stat·hœis]
city hall	**stadhuis**	[stat·hœis]
hotel	**hotel**	[hotəl]
bank	**bank**	[bank]
embassy	**ambassade**	[ambassadə]
travel agency	**reisagentskap**	[ræjs·aχentskap]
information office	**inligtingskantoor**	[inliχtiŋs·kantoər]
currency exchange	**wisselkantoor**	[vissəl·kantoər]
subway	**metro**	[metro]
hospital	**hospitaal**	[hospitāl]
gas station	**petrolstasie**	[petrol·stasi]
parking lot	**parkeerterrein**	[parkeər·terræjn]

30. Signs

signboard (store sign, etc.)	**reklamebord**	[reklamə·bort]
notice (door sign, etc.)	**kennisgewing**	[kɛnnis·χeviŋ]
poster	**plakkaat**	[plakkāt]
direction sign	**rigtingwyser**	[riχtiŋ·wajsər]
arrow (sign)	**pyl**	[pajl]
caution	**waarskuwing**	[vārskuviŋ]
warning sign	**waarskuwingsbord**	[vārskuviŋs·bort]

to warn (vt)	waarsku	[vãrsku]
rest day (weekly ~)	rusdag	[rusdaχ]
timetable (schedule)	diensrooster	[diŋs·roəstər]
opening hours	besigheidsure	[besiχæjts·urə]

WELCOME!	WELKOM!	[vɛlkom!]
ENTRANCE	INGANG	[inχaŋ]
EXIT	UITGANG	[œitχaŋ]

PUSH	STOOT	[stoət]
PULL	TREK	[trek]
OPEN	OOP	[oəp]
CLOSED	GESLUIT	[χeslœit]

| WOMEN | DAMES | [dames] |
| MEN | MANS | [maŋs] |

DISCOUNTS	AFSLAG	[afslaχ]
SALE	UITVERKOPING	[œitferkopiŋ]
NEW!	NUUT!	[nɪt!]
FREE	GRATIS	[χratis]

ATTENTION!	PAS OP!	[pas op!]
NO VACANCIES	VOLBESPREEK	[folbespreək]
RESERVED	BESPREEK	[bespreək]

| ADMINISTRATION | ADMINISTRASIE | [administrasi] |
| STAFF ONLY | SLEGS PERSONEEL | [sleχs personeəl] |

BEWARE OF THE DOG!	PAS OP VIR DIE HOND!	[pas op fir di hont!]
NO SMOKING	ROOK VERBODE	[roək ferbodə]
DO NOT TOUCH!	NIE AANRAAK NIE!	[ni ãnrãk ni!]

DANGEROUS	GEVAARLIK	[χefãrlik]
DANGER	GEVAAR	[χefãr]
HIGH VOLTAGE	HOOGSPANNING	[hoəχ·spanniŋ]
NO SWIMMING!	NIE SWEM NIE	[ni swem ni]
OUT OF ORDER	BUITE WERKING	[bœitə verkiŋ]

FLAMMABLE	ONTVLAMBAAR	[ontflambãr]
FORBIDDEN	VERBODE	[ferbodə]
NO TRESPASSING!	TOEGANG VERBODE!	[tuχaŋ ferbode!]
WET PAINT	NAT VERF	[nat ferf]

31. Shopping

to buy (purchase)	koop	[koəp]
purchase	aankoop	[ãnkoəp]
to go shopping	inkopies doen	[inkopis dun]
shopping	inkoop	[inkoəp]

to be open (ab. store)	**oop wees**	[oəp veəs]
to be closed	**toe wees**	[tu veəs]
footwear, shoes	**skoeisel**	[skuisəl]
clothes, clothing	**klere**	[klerə]
cosmetics	**kosmetika**	[kosmetika]
food products	**voedingsware**	[fudiŋs·warə]
gift, present	**present**	[present]
salesman	**verkoper**	[ferkopər]
saleswoman	**verkoopsdame**	[ferkoəps·damə]
check out, cash desk	**kassier**	[kassir]
mirror	**spieêl**	[spiɛl]
counter (store ~)	**toonbank**	[toən·bank]
fitting room	**paskamer**	[pas·kamər]
to try on	**aanpas**	[ānpas]
to fit (ab. dress, etc.)	**pas**	[pas]
to like (I like …)	**hou van**	[hæʊ fan]
price	**prys**	[prajs]
price tag	**pryskaartjie**	[prajs·kārki]
to cost (vt)	**kos**	[kos]
How much?	**Hoeveel?**	[hufeəl?]
discount	**afslag**	[afslaχ]
inexpensive (adj)	**billik**	[billik]
cheap (adj)	**goedkoop**	[χudkoəp]
expensive (adj)	**duur**	[dɪr]
It's expensive	**dis duur**	[dis dɪr]
rental (n)	**verhuur**	[ferhɪr]
to rent (~ a tuxedo)	**verhuur**	[ferhɪr]
credit (trade credit)	**krediet**	[kredit]
on credit (adv)	**op krediet**	[op kredit]

CLOTHING & ACCESSORIES

T&P Books Publishing

32. Outerwear. Coats

clothes	klere	[klerə]
outerwear	oorklere	[oərklerə]
winter clothing	winterklere	[vintər·klerə]

coat (overcoat)	jas	[jas]
fur coat	pelsjas	[pelʃas]
fur jacket	kort pelsjas	[kort pelʃas]
down coat	donsjas	[donʃas]

jacket (e.g., leather ~)	baadjie	[bādʒi]
raincoat (trenchcoat, etc.)	reënjas	[rɛɛnjas]
waterproof (adj)	waterdig	[vatərdəχ]

33. Men's & women's clothing

shirt (button shirt)	hemp	[hemp]
pants	broek	[bruk]
jeans	denimbroek	[denim·bruk]
suit jacket	baadjie	[bādʒi]
suit	pak	[pak]

dress (frock)	rok	[rok]
skirt	romp	[romp]
blouse	bloes	[blus]
knitted jacket (cardigan, etc.)	gebreide baadjie	[χebræjdə bādʒi]
jacket (of woman's suit)	baadjie	[bādʒi]

T-shirt	T-hemp	[te-hemp]
shorts (short trousers)	kortbroek	[kort·bruk]
tracksuit	sweetpak	[sweət·pak]
bathrobe	badjas	[batjas]
pajamas	pajama	[pajama]

sweater	trui	[trœi]
pullover	trui	[trœi]

vest	onderbaadjie	[ondər·bādʒi]
tailcoat	swaelstertbaadjie	[swaɛlstert·bādʒi]
tuxedo	aandpak	[āntpak]
uniform	uniform	[uniform]
workwear	werksklere	[verks·klerə]

| overalls | **oorpak** | [oərpak] |
| coat (e.g., doctor's smock) | **jas** | [jas] |

34. Clothing. Underwear

underwear	**onderklere**	[ondərklerə]
boxers, briefs	**onderbroek**	[ondərbruk]
panties	**onderbroek**	[ondərbruk]
undershirt (A-shirt)	**frokkie**	[frokki]
socks	**sokkies**	[sokkis]

nightgown	**nagrok**	[naχrok]
bra	**bra**	[bra]
knee highs (knee-high socks)	**kniekouse**	[kni·kæʊsə]
pantyhose	**kousbroek**	[kæʊsbruk]
stockings (thigh highs)	**kouse**	[kæʊsə]
bathing suit	**baaikostuum**	[bāj·kostɪm]

35. Headwear

hat	**hoed**	[hut]
fedora	**hoed**	[hut]
baseball cap	**bofbalpet**	[bofbal·pet]
flatcap	**pet**	[pet]

beret	**mus**	[mus]
hood	**kap**	[kap]
panama hat	**panamahoed**	[panama·hut]
knit cap (knitted hat)	**gebreide mus**	[χebræjdə mus]

| headscarf | **kopdoek** | [kopduk] |
| women's hat | **dameshoed** | [dames·hut] |

hard hat	**veiligheidshelm**	[fæjliχæjts·hɛlm]
garrison cap	**mus**	[mus]
helmet	**helmet**	[hɛlmet]

| derby | **bolhoed** | [bolhut] |
| top hat | **hoëhoed** | [hoɛhut] |

36. Footwear

footwear	**skoeisel**	[skuisəl]
shoes (men's shoes)	**mansskoene**	[maŋs·skunə]
shoes (women's shoes)	**damesskoene**	[dames·skunə]

| boots (e.g., cowboy ~) | laarse | [lãrsə] |
| slippers | pantoffels | [pantoffəls] |

tennis shoes (e.g., Nike ~)	tennisskoene	[tɛnnis·skunə]
sneakers	tekkies	[tɛkkis]
(e.g., Converse ~)		
sandals	sandale	[sandalə]

cobbler (shoe repairer)	skoenmaker	[skun·makər]
heel	hak	[hak]
pair (of shoes)	paar	[pãr]

| shoestring | skoenveter | [skun·fetər] |
| to lace (vt) | ryg | [rajχ] |

| shoehorn | skoenlepel | [skun·lepəl] |
| shoe polish | skoenpolitoer | [skun·politur] |

37. Personal accessories

gloves	handskoene	[handskunə]
mittens	duimhandskoene	[dœim·handskunə]
scarf (muffler)	serp	[serp]

glasses (eyeglasses)	bril	[bril]
frame (eyeglass ~)	raam	[rãm]
umbrella	sambreel	[sambreəl]
walking stick	wandelstok	[vandəl·stok]

| hairbrush | haarborsel | [hãr·borsəl] |
| fan | waaier | [vãjer] |

| tie (necktie) | das | [das] |
| bow tie | strikkie | [strikki] |

| suspenders | kruisbande | [krœis·bandə] |
| handkerchief | sakdoek | [sakduk] |

| comb | kam | [kam] |
| barrette | haarspeld | [hãrs·pɛlt] |

| hairpin | haarpen | [hãr·pen] |
| buckle | gespe | [χespə] |

| belt | belt | [bɛlt] |
| shoulder strap | skouerband | [skæʋer·bant] |

bag (handbag)	handsak	[hand·sak]
purse	beursie	[bøərsi]
backpack	rugsak	[ruχsak]

38. Clothing. Miscellaneous

fashion	**mode**	[modə]
in vogue (adj)	**in die mode**	[in di modə]
fashion designer	**modeontwerper**	[modə·ontwerpər]
collar	**kraag**	[krāχ]
pocket	**sak**	[sak]
pocket (as adj)	**sak-**	[sak-]
sleeve	**mou**	[mæʊ]
hanging loop	**lussie**	[lussi]
fly (on trousers)	**gulp**	[χulp]
zipper (fastener)	**ritssluiter**	[rits·slœitər]
fastener	**vasmaker**	[fasmakər]
button	**knoop**	[knoəp]
buttonhole	**knoopsgat**	[knoəps·χat]
to come off (ab. button)	**loskom**	[loskom]
to sew (vi, vt)	**naai**	[nāi]
to embroider (vi, vt)	**borduur**	[bordɪr]
embroidery	**borduurwerk**	[bordɪr·werk]
sewing needle	**naald**	[nālt]
thread	**garing**	[χariŋ]
seam	**soom**	[soəm]
to get dirty (vi)	**vuil word**	[fœil vort]
stain (mark, spot)	**vlek**	[flek]
to crease, crumple (vi)	**kreukel**	[krøəkəl]
to tear, to rip (vt)	**skeur**	[skøər]
clothes moth	**mot**	[mot]

39. Personal care. Cosmetics

toothpaste	**tandepasta**	[tandə·pasta]
toothbrush	**tandeborsel**	[tandə·borsəl]
to brush one's teeth	**tande borsel**	[tandə borsəl]
razor	**skeermes**	[skeər·mes]
shaving cream	**skeerroom**	[skeər·roəm]
to shave (vi)	**skeer**	[skeər]
soap	**seep**	[seəp]
shampoo	**sjampoe**	[ʃampu]
scissors	**skèr**	[skær]
nail file	**naelvyl**	[naɛl·fajl]
nail clippers	**naelknipper**	[naɛl·knippər]
tweezers	**haartangetjie**	[hārtaŋəki]

cosmetics	**kosmetika**	[kosmetika]
face mask	**gesigmasker**	[χesiχ·maskər]
manicure	**manikuur**	[manikɪr]
to have a manicure	**laat manikuur**	[lāt manikɪr]
pedicure	**voetbehandeling**	[fut·behandeliŋ]
make-up bag	**kosmetika tassie**	[kosmetika tassi]
face powder	**gesigpoeier**	[χesiχ·pujer]
powder compact	**poeierdosie**	[pujer·dosi]
blusher	**blosser**	[blossər]
perfume (bottled)	**parfuum**	[parfɪm]
toilet water (lotion)	**reukwater**	[røək·vatər]
lotion	**vloeiroom**	[flui·roəm]
cologne	**reukwater**	[røək·vatər]
eyeshadow	**oogskadu**	[oəχ·skadu]
eyeliner	**oogomlyner**	[oəχ·omlajnər]
mascara	**maskara**	[maskara]
lipstick	**lipstiffie**	[lip·stiffi]
nail polish, enamel	**naellak**	[naɛl·lak]
hair spray	**haarsproei**	[hārs·prui]
deodorant	**reukweermiddel**	[røək·veərmiddəl]
cream	**room**	[roəm]
face cream	**gesigroom**	[χesiχ·roəm]
hand cream	**handroom**	[hand·roəm]
anti-wrinkle cream	**antirimpelroom**	[antirimpəl·roəm]
day cream	**dagroom**	[daχ·roəm]
night cream	**nagroom**	[naχ·roəm]
day (as adj)	**dag-**	[daχ-]
night (as adj)	**nag-**	[naχ-]
tampon	**tampon**	[tampon]
toilet paper (toilet roll)	**toiletpapier**	[tojlet·papir]
hair dryer	**haardroër**	[hār·droɛr]

40. Watches. Clocks

watch (wristwatch)	**polshorlosie**	[pols·horlosi]
dial	**wyserplaat**	[vajsər·plāt]
hand (of clock, watch)	**wyster**	[vajstər]
metal watch band	**metaal horlosiebandjie**	[metāl horlosi·bandʒi]
watch strap	**horlosiebandjie**	[horlosi·bandʒi]
battery	**battery**	[battəraj]
to be dead (battery)	**pap wees**	[pap veəs]
to run fast	**voorloop**	[foərloəp]
to run slow	**agterloop**	[aχtərloəp]

wall clock	**muurhorlosie**	[mɪr·horlosi]
hourglass	**uurglas**	[ɪr·χlas]
sundial	**sonwyser**	[son·wajsər]
alarm clock	**wekker**	[vɛkkər]
watchmaker	**horlosiemaker**	[horlosi·makər]
to repair (vt)	**herstel**	[herstəl]

EVERYDAY EXPERIENCE

T&P Books Publishing

money	geld	[χɛlt]
currency exchange	valutaruil	[faluta·rœil]
exchange rate	wisselkoers	[vissəl·kurs]
ATM	OTM	[o·te·em]
coin	muntstuk	[muntstuk]

dollar	dollar	[dollar]
euro	euro	[øəro]

lira	lira	[lira]
Deutschmark	Duitse mark	[dœitsə mark]
franc	frank	[frank]
pound sterling	pond sterling	[pont sterliŋ]
yen	yen	[jɛn]

debt	skuld	[skult]
debtor	skuldenaar	[skuldenãr]
to lend (money)	uitleen	[œitleən]
to borrow (vi, vt)	leen	[leən]

bank	bank	[bank]
account	rekening	[rekəniŋ]
to deposit (vt)	deponeer	[deponeər]
to withdraw (vt)	trek	[trek]

credit card	kredietkaart	[kredit·kãrt]
cash	kontant	[kontant]
check	tjek	[ʧek]
checkbook	tjekboek	[ʧek·buk]

wallet	beursie	[bøərsi]
change purse	muntstukbeursie	[muntstuk·bøərsi]
safe	brandkas	[brant·kas]

heir	erfgenaam	[ɛrfχənãm]
inheritance	erfenis	[ɛrfenis]
fortune (wealth)	fortuin	[fortœin]

lease	huur	[hɪr]
rent (money)	huur	[hɪr]
to rent (sth from sb)	huur	[hɪr]

price	prys	[prajs]
cost	prys	[prajs]

sum	**som**	[som]
to spend (vt)	**spandeer**	[spandeər]
expenses	**onkoste**	[onkostə]
to economize (vi, vt)	**besuinig**	[besœinəχ]
economical	**ekonomies**	[ɛkonomis]
to pay (vi, vt)	**betaal**	[betāl]
payment	**betaling**	[betaliŋ]
change (give the ~)	**wisselgeld**	[vissəl·χɛlt]
tax	**belasting**	[belastiŋ]
fine	**boete**	[butə]
to fine (vt)	**beboet**	[bebut]

42. Post. Postal service

post office	**poskantoor**	[pos·kantoər]
mail (letters, etc.)	**pos**	[pos]
mailman	**posbode**	[pos·bodə]
opening hours	**besigheidsure**	[besiχæjts·urə]
letter	**brief**	[brif]
registered letter	**geregistreerde brief**	[χereχistreərdə brif]
postcard	**poskaart**	[pos·kārt]
telegram	**telegram**	[teleχram]
package (parcel)	**pakkie**	[pakki]
money transfer	**geldoorplasing**	[χɛld·oərplasiŋ]
to receive (vt)	**ontvang**	[ontfaŋ]
to send (vt)	**stuur**	[stIr]
sending	**versending**	[fersendiŋ]
address	**adres**	[adres]
ZIP code	**poskode**	[pos·kodə]
sender	**sender**	[sendər]
receiver	**ontvanger**	[ontfaŋər]
name (first name)	**voornaam**	[foərnām]
surname (last name)	**van**	[fan]
postage rate	**postarief**	[pos·tarif]
standard (adj)	**standaard**	[standārt]
economical (adj)	**ekonomies**	[ɛkonomis]
weight	**gewig**	[χevəχ]
to weigh (~ letters)	**weeg**	[veəχ]
envelope	**koevert**	[kufert]
postage stamp	**posseël**	[pos·seɛl]

43. Banking

bank	**bank**	[bank]
branch (of bank, etc.)	**tak**	[tak]
bank clerk, consultant	**bankklerk**	[bank·klerk]
manager (director)	**bestuurder**	[bestɪrdər]
bank account	**bankrekening**	[bank·rekəniŋ]
account number	**rekeningnommer**	[rekəniŋ·nommər]
checking account	**tjekrekening**	[ʧek·rekəniŋ]
savings account	**spaarrekening**	[spār·rekəniŋ]
to close the account	**die rekening sluit**	[di rekəniŋ slœit]
to withdraw (vt)	**trek**	[trek]
deposit	**deposito**	[deposito]
wire transfer	**telegrafiese oorplasing**	[teleχrafisə oərplasiŋ]
to wire, to transfer	**oorplaas**	[oərplās]
sum	**som**	[som]
How much?	**Hoeveel?**	[hufeəl?]
signature	**handtekening**	[hand·tekəniŋ]
to sign (vt)	**onderteken**	[ondərtekən]
credit card	**kredietkaart**	[kredit·kārt]
code (PIN code)	**kode**	[kodə]
credit card number	**kredietkaartnommer**	[kredit·kārt·nommər]
ATM	**OTM**	[o·te·em]
check	**tjek**	[ʧek]
checkbook	**tjekboek**	[ʧek·buk]
loan (bank ~)	**lening**	[leniŋ]
guarantee	**waarborg**	[vārborχ]

44. Telephone. Phone conversation

telephone	**telefoon**	[telefoən]
cell phone	**selfoon**	[sɛlfoən]
answering machine	**antwoordmasjien**	[antwoərt·maʃin]
to call (by phone)	**bel**	[bəl]
phone call	**oproep**	[oprup]
Hello!	**Hallo!**	[hallo!]
to ask (vt)	**vra**	[fra]
to answer (vi, vt)	**antwoord**	[antwoərt]

to hear (vt)	**hoor**	[hoər]
well (adv)	**goed**	[χut]
not well (adv)	**nie goed nie**	[ni χut ni]
noises (interference)	**steurings**	[støəriŋs]
receiver	**gehoorstuk**	[χehoərstuk]
to pick up (~ the phone)	**optel**	[optəl]
to hang up (~ the phone)	**afskakel**	[afskakəl]
busy (engaged)	**besig**	[besəχ]
to ring (ab. phone)	**lui**	[lœi]
telephone book	**telefoongids**	[telefoən·χids]
local (adj)	**lokale**	[lokalə]
local call	**lokale oproep**	[lokalə oprup]
long distance (~ call)	**langafstand**	[lanχ·afstant]
long-distance call	**langafstand oproep**	[lanχ·afstant oprup]
international (adj)	**internasionale**	[internaʃionalə]
international call	**internasionale oproep**	[internaʃionalə oprup]

45. Cell phone

cell phone	**selfoon**	[sɛlfoən]
display	**skerm**	[skerm]
button	**knoppie**	[knoppi]
SIM card	**SIMkaart**	[sim·kārt]
battery	**battery**	[battəraj]
to be dead (battery)	**pap wees**	[pap veəs]
charger	**batterylaaier**	[battəraj·lajer]
menu	**spyskaart**	[spajs·kārt]
settings	**instellings**	[instɛlliŋs]
tune (melody)	**wysie**	[vajsi]
to select (vt)	**kies**	[kis]
calculator	**sakrekenaar**	[sakrekənār]
voice mail	**stempos**	[stem·pos]
alarm clock	**wekker**	[vɛkkər]
contacts	**kontakte**	[kontaktə]
SMS (text message)	**SMS**	[es·em·es]
subscriber	**intekenaar**	[intekənār]

46. Stationery

ballpoint pen	**bolpen**	[bol·pen]
fountain pen	**vulpen**	[ful·pen]

pencil	**potlood**	[potloət]
highlighter	**merkpen**	[merk·pen]
felt-tip pen	**viltpen**	[filt·pen]

| notepad | **notaboekie** | [nota·buki] |
| agenda (diary) | **dagboek** | [daχ·buk] |

ruler	**liniaal**	[liniãl]
calculator	**sakrekenaar**	[sakrekənãr]
eraser	**uitveêr**	[œitfeɛr]
thumbtack	**duimspyker**	[dœim·spajkər]
paper clip	**skuifspeld**	[skœif·spɛlt]

glue	**gom**	[χom]
stapler	**krammasjien**	[kram·maʃin]
hole punch	**ponsmasjien**	[pɔŋs·maʃin]
pencil sharpener	**skerpmaker**	[skerp·makər]

47. Foreign languages

language	**taal**	[tãl]
foreign (adj)	**vreemd**	[freəmt]
foreign language	**vreemde taal**	[freəmdə tãl]
to study (vt)	**studeer**	[studeər]
to learn (language, etc.)	**leer**	[leər]

to read (vi, vt)	**lees**	[leəs]
to speak (vi, vt)	**praat**	[prãt]
to understand (vt)	**verstaan**	[ferstãn]
to write (vt)	**skryf**	[skrajf]

fast (adv)	**vinnig**	[finnəχ]
slowly (adv)	**stadig**	[stadəχ]
fluently (adv)	**vlot**	[flot]

rules	**reêls**	[reɛls]
grammar	**grammatika**	[χrammatika]
vocabulary	**woordeskat**	[voərdeskat]
phonetics	**fonetika**	[fonetika]

textbook	**handboek**	[hand·buk]
dictionary	**woordeboek**	[voərdə·buk]
teach-yourself book	**selfstudie boek**	[sɛlfstudi buk]
phrasebook	**taalgids**	[tãl·χids]

cassette, tape	**kasset**	[kasset]
videotape	**videoband**	[video·bant]
CD, compact disc	**CD**	[se·de]
DVD	**DVD**	[de·fe·de]
alphabet	**alfabet**	[alfabet]

to spell (vt)	**spel**	[spel]
pronunciation	**uitspraak**	[œitsprāk]
accent	**aksent**	[aksent]
word	**woord**	[voərt]
meaning	**betekenis**	[betekənis]
course (e.g., a French ~)	**kursus**	[kursus]
to sign up	**inskryf**	[inskrajf]
teacher	**onderwyser**	[ondərwajsər]
translation (process)	**vertaling**	[fertaliŋ]
translation (text, etc.)	**vertaling**	[fertaliŋ]
translator	**vertaler**	[fertalər]
interpreter	**tolk**	[tolk]
polyglot	**poliglot**	[poliχlot]
memory	**geheue**	[χəhøə]

MEALS. RESTAURANT

T&P Books Publishing

48. Table setting

spoon	**lepel**	[lepəl]
knife	**mes**	[mes]
fork	**vurk**	[furk]
cup (e.g., coffee ~)	**koppie**	[koppi]
plate (dinner ~)	**bord**	[bort]
saucer	**piering**	[piriŋ]
napkin (on table)	**servet**	[serfət]
toothpick	**tandestokkie**	[tandə·stokki]

49. Restaurant

restaurant	**restaurant**	[restourant]
coffee house	**koffiekroeg**	[koffi·kruχ]
pub, bar	**kroeg**	[kruχ]
tearoom	**teekamer**	[teə·kamər]
waiter	**kelner**	[kɛlnər]
waitress	**kelnerin**	[kɛlnərin]
bartender	**kroegman**	[kruχman]
menu	**spyskaart**	[spajs·kārt]
wine list	**wyn**	[vajn]
to book a table	**wynkaart**	[vajn·kārt]
course, dish	**gereg**	[χerəχ]
to order (meal)	**bestel**	[bestəl]
to make an order	**bestel**	[bestəl]
aperitif	**drankie**	[dranki]
appetizer	**voorgereg**	[foərχerəχ]
dessert	**nagereg**	[naχerəχ]
check	**rekening**	[rekəniŋ]
to pay the check	**die rekening betaal**	[di rekeniŋ betāl]
to give change	**kleingeld gee**	[klæjn·χɛlt χeə]
tip	**fooitjie**	[fojki]

50. Meals

food	**kos**	[kos]
to eat (vi, vt)	**eet**	[eət]

breakfast	ontbyt	[ontbajt]
to have breakfast	ontbyt	[ontbajt]
lunch	middagete	[middaχ·etə]
to have lunch	gaan eet	[χān eət]
dinner	aandete	[āndetə]
to have dinner	aandete gebruik	[āndetə χebrœik]
appetite	aptyt	[aptajt]
Enjoy your meal!	Smaaklike ete!	[smāklikə etə!]
to open (~ a bottle)	oopmaak	[oəpmāk]
to spill (liquid)	mors	[mors]
to spill out (vi)	mors	[mors]
to boil (vi)	kook	[koək]
to boil (vt)	kook	[koək]
boiled (~ water)	gekook	[χekoək]
to chill, cool down (vt)	laat afkoel	[lāt afkul]
to chill (vi)	afkoel	[afkul]
taste, flavor	smaak	[smāk]
aftertaste	nasmaak	[nasmāk]
to slim down (lose weight)	vermaer	[fermaər]
diet	dieet	[diət]
vitamin	vitamien	[fitamin]
calorie	kalorie	[kalori]
vegetarian (n)	vegetariër	[feχetariɛr]
vegetarian (adj)	vegetaries	[feχetaris]
fats (nutrient)	vette	[fɛttə]
proteins	proteïen	[proteïen]
carbohydrates	koolhidrate	[koəlhidratə]
slice (of lemon, ham)	snytjie	[snajki]
piece (of cake, pie)	stuk	[stuk]
crumb	krummel	[krumməl]
(of bread, cake, etc.)		

51. Cooked dishes

course, dish	gereg	[χerəχ]
cuisine	kookkuns	[koək·kuns]
recipe	resep	[resep]
portion	porsie	[porsi]
salad	slaai	[slāi]
soup	sop	[sop]
clear soup (broth)	helder sop	[hɛldər sop]
sandwich (bread)	toebroodjie	[tubroədʒi]

fried eggs	gabakte eiers	[χabaktə æjers]
hamburger (beefburger)	hamburger	[hamburχər]
beefsteak	biefstuk	[bifstuk]

side dish	sygereg	[saj·χerəχ]
spaghetti	spaghetti	[spaχɛtti]
mashed potatoes	kapokaartappels	[kapok·ārtappəls]
pizza	pizza	[pizza]
porridge (oatmeal, etc.)	pap	[pap]
omelet	omelet	[oməlet]

boiled (e.g., ~ beef)	gekook	[χekoək]
smoked (adj)	gerook	[χeroək]
fried (adj)	gebak	[χebak]
dried (adj)	gedroog	[χedroəχ]
frozen (adj)	gevries	[χefris]
pickled (adj)	gepiekel	[χepikəl]

sweet (sugary)	soet	[sut]
salty (adj)	sout	[sæʊt]
cold (adj)	koud	[kæʊt]
hot (adj)	warm	[varm]
bitter (adj)	bitter	[bittər]
tasty (adj)	smaaklik	[smāklik]

to cook in boiling water	kook in water	[koək in vatər]
to cook (dinner)	kook	[koək]
to fry (vt)	braai	[braj]
to heat up (food)	opwarm	[opwarm]

to salt (vt)	sout	[sæʊt]
to pepper (vt)	peper	[pepər]
to grate (vt)	rasp	[rasp]
peel (n)	skil	[skil]
to peel (vt)	skil	[skil]

52. Food

meat	vleis	[flæjs]
chicken	hoender	[hundər]
Rock Cornish hen (poussin)	braaikuiken	[brāj·kœiken]
duck	eend	[eent]
goose	gans	[χaŋs]
game	wild	[vilt]
turkey	kalkoen	[kalkun]

pork	varkvleis	[fark·flæjs]
veal	kalfsvleis	[kalfs·flæjs]
lamb	lamsvleis	[lams·flæjs]

| beef | beesvleis | [beəs·flæjs] |
| rabbit | konynvleis | [konajn·flæjs] |

sausage (bologna, pepperoni, etc.)	wors	[vors]
vienna sausage (frankfurter)	Weense worsie	[veɛŋsə vorsi]
bacon	spek	[spek]
ham	ham	[ham]
gammon	gerookte ham	[xeroəktə ham]

pâté	patee	[pateə]
liver	lewer	[levər]
hamburger (ground beef)	maalvleis	[māl·flæjs]
tongue	tong	[toŋ]

egg	eier	[æjer]
eggs	eiers	[æjers]
egg white	eierwit	[æjer·wit]
egg yolk	dooier	[dojer]

fish	vis	[fis]
seafood	seekos	[seə·kos]
crustaceans	skaaldiere	[skāldirə]
caviar	kaviaar	[kafiār]

crab	krab	[krap]
shrimp	garnaal	[xarnāl]
oyster	oester	[ustər]
spiny lobster	seekreef	[seə·kreəf]
octopus	seekat	[seə·kat]
squid	pylinkvis	[pajl·inkfis]

sturgeon	steur	[støər]
salmon	salm	[salm]
halibut	heilbot	[hæjlbot]

cod	kabeljou	[kabeljæʊ]
mackerel	makriel	[makril]
tuna	tuna	[tuna]
eel	paling	[paliŋ]

trout	forel	[forəl]
sardine	sardyn	[sardajn]
pike	varswatersnoek	[farswatər·snuk]
herring	haring	[hariŋ]

bread	brood	[broət]
cheese	kaas	[kās]
sugar	suiker	[sœikər]
salt	sout	[sæʊt]
rice	rys	[rajs]

pasta (macaroni)	**pasta**	[pasta]
noodles	**noedels**	[nudɛls]
butter	**botter**	[bottər]
vegetable oil	**plantaardige olie**	[plantārdiχə oli]
sunflower oil	**sonblomolie**	[sonblom·oli]
margarine	**margarien**	[marχarin]
olives	**olywe**	[olajvə]
olive oil	**olyfolie**	[olajf·oli]
milk	**melk**	[melk]
condensed milk	**kondensmelk**	[kondɛŋs·melk]
yogurt	**jogurt**	[joχurt]
sour cream	**suurroom**	[sɪr·roəm]
cream (of milk)	**room**	[roəm]
mayonnaise	**mayonnaise**	[majonɛs]
buttercream	**crème**	[krɛm]
cereal grains (wheat, etc.)	**ontbytgraan**	[ontbajt·χrān]
flour	**meelblom**	[meəl·blom]
canned food	**blikkieskos**	[blikkis·kos]
cornflakes	**mielievlokkies**	[mili·flokkis]
honey	**heuning**	[høəniŋ]
jam	**konfyt**	[konfajt]
chewing gum	**kougom**	[kæʊχom]

53. Drinks

water	**water**	[vatər]
drinking water	**drinkwater**	[drink·vatər]
mineral water	**mineraalwater**	[minerāl·vatər]
still (adj)	**sonder gas**	[sondər χas]
carbonated (adj)	**soda-**	[soda-]
sparkling (adj)	**bruis-**	[brœis-]
ice	**ys**	[ajs]
with ice	**met ys**	[met ajs]
non-alcoholic (adj)	**nie-alkoholies**	[ni-alkoholis]
soft drink	**koeldrank**	[kul·drank]
refreshing drink	**verfrissende drank**	[ferfrissendə drank]
lemonade	**limonade**	[limonadə]
liquors	**likeure**	[likøərə]
wine	**wyn**	[vajn]
white wine	**witwyn**	[vit·vajn]
red wine	**rooiwyn**	[roj·vajn]

liqueur	**likeur**	[likøər]
champagne	**sjampanje**	[ʃampanje]
vermouth	**vermoet**	[fermut]

whiskey	**whisky**	[vhiskaj]
vodka	**vodka**	[fodka]
gin	**jenever**	[jenefər]
cognac	**brandewyn**	[brandə·vajn]
rum	**rum**	[rum]

coffee	**koffie**	[koffi]
black coffee	**swart koffie**	[swart koffi]
coffee with milk	**koffie met melk**	[koffi met melk]
cappuccino	**capuccino**	[kaputʃino]
instant coffee	**poeierkoffie**	[pujer·koffi]

milk	**melk**	[melk]
cocktail	**mengeldrankie**	[menχəl·dranki]
milkshake	**melkskommel**	[melk·skomməl]

juice	**sap**	[sap]
tomato juice	**tamatiesap**	[tamati·sap]
orange juice	**lemoensap**	[lemoən·sap]
freshly squeezed juice	**vars geparste sap**	[fars χeparstə sap]

beer	**bier**	[bir]
light beer	**ligte bier**	[liχtə bir]
dark beer	**donker bier**	[donkər bir]

tea	**tee**	[teə]
black tea	**swart tee**	[swart teə]
green tea	**groen tee**	[χrun teə]

54. Vegetables

| vegetables | **groente** | [χruntə] |
| greens | **groente** | [χruntə] |

tomato	**tamatie**	[tamati]
cucumber	**komkommer**	[komkommər]
carrot	**wortel**	[vortəl]
potato	**aartappel**	[ārtappəl]
onion	**ui**	[œi]
garlic	**knoffel**	[knoffəl]

cabbage	**kool**	[koəl]
cauliflower	**blomkool**	[blom·koəl]
Brussels sprouts	**Brusselspruite**	[brussɛl·sprœitə]
broccoli	**broccoli**	[brokoli]
beetroot	**beet**	[beət]

eggplant	eiervrug	[æjerfruχ]
zucchini	vingerskorsie	[fiŋər·skorsi]
pumpkin	pampoen	[pampun]
turnip	raap	[răp]

parsley	pietersielie	[pitərsili]
dill	dille	[dillə]
lettuce	slaai	[slăi]
celery	seldery	[selderaj]
asparagus	aspersie	[aspersi]
spinach	spinasie	[spinasi]

pea	ertjie	[ɛrki]
beans	boontjies	[boənkis]
corn (maize)	mielie	[mili]
kidney bean	nierboontjie	[nir·boənki]

bell pepper	paprika	[paprika]
radish	radys	[radajs]
artichoke	artisjok	[artiʃok]

55. Fruits. Nuts

fruit	vrugte	[fruχtə]
apple	appel	[appəl]
pear	peer	[peər]
lemon	suurlemoen	[sɪr·lemun]
orange	lemoen	[lemun]
strawberry (garden ~)	aarbei	[ārbæj]

mandarin	nartjie	[narki]
plum	pruim	[prœim]
peach	perske	[perskə]
apricot	appelkoos	[appɛlkoəs]
raspberry	framboos	[framboəs]
pineapple	pynappel	[pajnappəl]

banana	piesang	[pisaŋ]
watermelon	waatlemoen	[vātlemun]
grape	druif	[drœif]
cherry	kersie	[kersi]
sour cherry	suurkersie	[sɪr·kersi]
sweet cherry	soetkersie	[sut·kersi]
melon	spanspek	[spaŋspek]

grapefruit	pomelo	[pomelo]
avocado	avokado	[afokado]
papaya	papaja	[papaja]
mango	mango	[manχo]
pomegranate	granaat	[χranãt]

redcurrant	rooi aalbessie	[roj ālbɛssi]
blackcurrant	swartbessie	[swartbɛssi]
gooseberry	appelliefie	[appɛllifi]
bilberry	bosbessie	[bosbɛssi]
blackberry	braambessie	[brāmbɛssi]

raisin	rosyntjie	[rosajnki]
fig	vy	[faj]
date	dadel	[dadəl]

peanut	grondboontjie	[xront·boənki]
almond	amandel	[amandəl]
walnut	okkerneut	[okkər·nøət]
hazelnut	haselneut	[hasɛl·nøət]
coconut	klapper	[klappər]
pistachios	pistachio	[pistatʃio]

56. Bread. Candy

bakers' confectionery (pastry)	soet gebak	[sut xebak]
bread	brood	[broət]
cookies	koekies	[kukis]

chocolate (n)	sjokolade	[ʃokoladə]
chocolate (as adj)	sjokolade	[ʃokoladə]
candy (wrapped)	lekkers	[lɛkkərs]
cake (e.g., cupcake)	koek	[kuk]
cake (e.g., birthday ~)	koek	[kuk]

| pie (e.g., apple ~) | pastei | [pastæj] |
| filling (for cake, pie) | vulsel | [fulsəl] |

jam (whole fruit jam)	konfyt	[konfajt]
marmalade	marmelade	[marmeladə]
waffles	wafels	[vafɛls]
ice-cream	roomys	[roəm·ajs]
pudding	poeding	[pudiŋ]

57. Spices

salt	sout	[sæʊt]
salty (adj)	sout	[sæʊt]
to salt (vt)	sout	[sæʊt]

black pepper	swart peper	[swart pepər]
red pepper (milled ~)	rooi peper	[roj pepər]
mustard	mosterd	[mostert]

horseradish	**peperwortel**	[peper·wortəl]
condiment	**smaakmiddel**	[smāk·middəl]
spice	**spesery**	[spesəraj]
sauce	**sous**	[sæʊs]
vinegar	**asyn**	[asajn]

anise	**anys**	[anajs]
basil	**basilikum**	[basilikum]
cloves	**naeltjies**	[naɛlkis]
ginger	**gemmer**	[χɛmmər]
coriander	**koljander**	[koljandər]
cinnamon	**kaneel**	[kaneəl]

sesame	**sesamsaad**	[sesam·sāt]
bay leaf	**lourierblaar**	[læʊrir·blār]
paprika	**paprika**	[paprika]
caraway	**komynsaad**	[komajnsāt]
saffron	**saffraan**	[saffrān]

PERSONAL
INFORMATION. FAMILY

T&P Books Publishing

58. Personal information. Forms

name (first name)	**voornaam**	[foərnãm]
surname (last name)	**van**	[fan]
date of birth	**geboortedatum**	[χeboərtə·datum]
place of birth	**geboorteplek**	[χeboərtə·plek]
nationality	**nasionaliteit**	[naʃionalitæjt]
place of residence	**woonplek**	[voən·plek]
country	**land**	[lant]
profession (occupation)	**beroep**	[berup]
gender, sex	**geslag**	[χeslaχ]
height	**lengte**	[leŋtə]
weight	**gewig**	[χevəχ]

59. Family members. Relatives

mother	**moeder**	[mudər]
father	**vader**	[fadər]
son	**seun**	[søən]
daughter	**dogter**	[doχtər]
younger daughter	**jonger dogter**	[joŋər doχtər]
younger son	**jonger seun**	[joŋər søən]
eldest daughter	**oudste dogter**	[æʊdstə doχtər]
eldest son	**oudste seun**	[æʊdstə søən]
brother	**broer**	[brur]
elder brother	**ouer broer**	[æʊer brur]
younger brother	**jonger broer**	[joŋər brur]
sister	**suster**	[sustər]
elder sister	**ouer suster**	[æʊer sustər]
younger sister	**jonger suster**	[joŋər sustər]
cousin (masc.)	**neef**	[neəf]
cousin (fem.)	**neef**	[neəf]
mom, mommy	**ma**	[ma]
dad, daddy	**pa**	[pa]
parents	**ouers**	[æʊers]
child	**kind**	[kint]
children	**kinders**	[kindərs]
grandmother	**ouma**	[æʊma]

grandfather	oupa	[æʊpa]
grandson	kleinseun	[klæjn·søən]
granddaughter	kleindogter	[klæjn·doχtər]
grandchildren	kleinkinders	[klæjn·kindərs]

uncle	oom	[oəm]
aunt	tante	[tantə]
nephew	neef	[neəf]
niece	nig	[niχ]

mother-in-law (wife's mother)	skoonma	[skoən·ma]
father-in-law (husband's father)	skoonpa	[skoən·pa]
son-in-law (daughter's husband)	skoonseun	[skoən·søən]
stepmother	stiefma	[stifma]
stepfather	stiefpa	[stifpa]

infant	baba	[baba]
baby (infant)	baba	[baba]
little boy, kid	seuntjie	[søənki]

wife	vrou	[fræʊ]
husband	man	[man]
spouse (husband)	eggenoot	[εχχenoət]
spouse (wife)	eggenote	[εχχenotə]

married (masc.)	getroud	[χetræʊt]
married (fem.)	getroud	[χetræʊt]
single (unmarried)	ongetroud	[onχətræʊt]
bachelor	vrygesel	[frajχesəl]
divorced (masc.)	geskei	[χeskæj]
widow	weduwee	[veduveə]
widower	wedunaar	[vedunãr]

relative	familielid	[famililit]
close relative	na familie	[na famili]
distant relative	ver familie	[fer famili]
relatives	familielede	[famililedə]

orphan (boy or girl)	weeskind	[veəskint]
guardian (of a minor)	voog	[foəχ]
to adopt (a boy)	aanneem	[ãnneəm]
to adopt (a girl)	aanneem	[ãnneəm]

60. Friends. Coworkers

| friend (masc.) | vriend | [frint] |
| friend (fem.) | vriendin | [frindin] |

friendship	**vriendskap**	[frindskap]
to be friends	**bevriend wees**	[befrint veəs]
buddy (masc.)	**maat**	[māt]
buddy (fem.)	**vriendin**	[frindin]
partner	**maat**	[māt]
chief (boss)	**baas**	[bās]
superior (n)	**baas**	[bās]
owner, proprietor	**eienaar**	[æjenār]
subordinate (n)	**ondergeskikte**	[ondərχeskiktə]
colleague	**kollega**	[kolleχa]
acquaintance (person)	**kennis**	[kɛnnis]
fellow traveler	**medereisiger**	[medə·ræjsiχər]
classmate	**klasmaat**	[klas·māt]
neighbor (masc.)	**buurman**	[bɪrman]
neighbor (fem.)	**buurvrou**	[bɪrfræʊ]
neighbors	**bure**	[burə]

HUMAN BODY. MEDICINE

T&P Books Publishing

61. Head

head	**kop**	[kop]
face	**gesig**	[χesəχ]
nose	**neus**	[nøəs]
mouth	**mond**	[mont]

eye	**oog**	[oəχ]
eyes	**oë**	[oɛ]
pupil	**pupil**	[pupil]
eyebrow	**wenkbrou**	[vɛnk·bræʋ]
eyelash	**ooghaar**	[oəχ·hār]
eyelid	**ooglid**	[oəχ·lit]

tongue	**tong**	[toŋ]
tooth	**tand**	[tant]
lips	**lippe**	[lippə]
cheekbones	**wangbene**	[vaŋ·benə]
gum	**tandvleis**	[tand·flæjs]
palate	**verhemelte**	[fer·hemɛltə]

nostrils	**neusgate**	[nøəsχatə]
chin	**ken**	[ken]
jaw	**kakebeen**	[kakebeən]
cheek	**wang**	[vaŋ]

forehead	**voorhoof**	[foərhoəf]
temple	**slaap**	[slāp]
ear	**oor**	[oər]
back of the head	**agterkop**	[aχtərkop]
neck	**nek**	[nek]
throat	**keel**	[keəl]

hair	**haar**	[hār]
hairstyle	**kapsel**	[kapsəl]
haircut	**haarstyl**	[hārstajl]
wig	**pruik**	[prœik]

mustache	**snor**	[snor]
beard	**baard**	[bārt]
to have (a beard, etc.)	**dra**	[dra]
braid	**vlegsel**	[fleχsəl]
sideburns	**bakkebaarde**	[bakkəbārdə]

red-haired (adj)	**rooiharig**	[roj·harəχ]
gray (hair)	**grys**	[χrajs]

bald (adj)	**kaal**	[kāl]
bald patch	**kaal plek**	[kāl plek]
ponytail	**poniestert**	[poni·stert]
bangs	**gordyntjiekapsel**	[xordajnki·kapsəl]

62. Human body

hand	**hand**	[hant]
arm	**arm**	[arm]
finger	**vinger**	[fiŋər]
toe	**toon**	[toən]
thumb	**duim**	[dœim]
little finger	**pinkie**	[pinki]
nail	**nael**	[naəl]
fist	**vuis**	[fœis]
palm	**palm**	[palm]
wrist	**pols**	[pols]
forearm	**voorarm**	[foərarm]
elbow	**elmboog**	[ɛlmboəx]
shoulder	**skouer**	[skæʊər]
leg	**been**	[beən]
foot	**voet**	[fut]
knee	**knie**	[kni]
calf (part of leg)	**kuit**	[kœit]
hip	**heup**	[høəp]
heel	**hakskeen**	[hak·skeən]
body	**liggaam**	[lixxām]
stomach	**maag**	[māx]
chest	**bors**	[bors]
breast	**bors**	[bors]
flank	**sy**	[saj]
back	**rug**	[rux]
lower back	**lae rug**	[laə rux]
waist	**middel**	[middəl]
navel (belly button)	**naeltjie**	[naɛlki]
buttocks	**boude**	[bæʊdə]
bottom	**sitvlak**	[sitflak]
beauty mark	**moesie**	[musi]
birthmark (café au lait spot)	**moedervlek**	[mudər·flek]
tattoo	**tatoe**	[tatu]
scar	**litteken**	[littekən]

63. Diseases

sickness	siekte	[siktə]
to be sick	siek wees	[sik veəs]
health	gesondheid	[χesonthæjt]

runny nose (coryza)	loopneus	[loəpnøəs]
tonsillitis	keelontsteking	[keəl·ontstekiŋ]
cold (illness)	verkoue	[ferkæʊə]

bronchitis	bronchitis	[bronχitis]
pneumonia	longontsteking	[loŋ·ontstekiŋ]
flu, influenza	griep	[χrip]

nearsighted (adj)	bysiende	[bajsində]
farsighted (adj)	versiende	[fersində]
strabismus (crossed eyes)	skeelheid	[skeəlhæjt]
cross-eyed (adj)	skeel	[skeəl]
cataract	katarak	[katarak]
glaucoma	gloukoom	[χlæʊkoəm]

stroke	beroerte	[berurtə]
heart attack	hartaanval	[hart·ānfal]
myocardial infarction	hartinfark	[hart·infark]
paralysis	verlamming	[ferlammiŋ]
to paralyze (vt)	verlam	[ferlam]

allergy	allergie	[allerχi]
asthma	asma	[asma]
diabetes	suikersiekte	[sœikər·siktə]

| toothache | tandpyn | [tand·pajn] |
| caries | tandbederf | [tand·bederf] |

diarrhea	diarree	[diarreə]
constipation	hardlywigheid	[hardlajviχæjt]
stomach upset	maagongesteldheid	[māχ·oŋəstɛldhæjt]
food poisoning	voedselvergiftiging	[fudsəl·ferχiftəχiŋ]
to get food poisoning	voedselvergiftiging kry	[fudsəl·ferχiftəχiŋ kraj]

arthritis	artritis	[artritis]
rickets	Engelse siekte	[ɛŋəlsə siktə]
rheumatism	reumatiek	[røəmatik]
atherosclerosis	artrosklerose	[artrosklerosə]

gastritis	maagontsteking	[māχ·ontstekiŋ]
appendicitis	blindedermontsteking	[blindəderm·ontstekiŋ]
cholecystitis	galblaasontsteking	[χalblās·ontstekiŋ]
ulcer	maagsweer	[māχsweər]
measles	masels	[masɛls]
rubella (German measles)	Duitse masels	[dœitsə masɛls]

| jaundice | **geelsug** | [χeəlsuχ] |
| hepatitis | **hepatitis** | [hepatitis] |

schizophrenia	**skisofrenie**	[skisofreni]
rabies (hydrophobia)	**hondsdolheid**	[hondsdolhæjt]
neurosis	**neurose**	[nøərosə]
concussion	**harsingskudding**	[harsiŋ·skuddiŋ]

cancer	**kanker**	[kankər]
sclerosis	**sklerose**	[sklerosə]
multiple sclerosis	**veelvuldige sklerose**	[feəlfuldiχə sklerosə]

alcoholism	**alkoholisme**	[alkoholismə]
alcoholic (n)	**alkoholikus**	[alkoholikus]
syphilis	**sifilis**	[sifilis]
AIDS	**VIGS**	[vigs]

tumor	**tumor**	[tumor]
malignant (adj)	**kwaadaardig**	[kwādārdəχ]
benign (adj)	**goedaardig**	[χudārdəχ]

fever	**koors**	[koərs]
malaria	**malaria**	[malaria]
gangrene	**gangreen**	[χanχreən]
seasickness	**seesiekte**	[seə·siktə]
epilepsy	**epilepsie**	[ɛpilepsi]

epidemic	**epidemie**	[ɛpidemi]
typhus	**tifus**	[tifus]
tuberculosis	**tuberkulose**	[tuberkulosə]
cholera	**cholera**	[χolera]
plague (bubonic ~)	**pes**	[pes]

64. Symptoms. Treatments. Part 1

symptom	**simptoom**	[simptoəm]
temperature	**temperatuur**	[temperatɪr]
high temperature (fever)	**koors**	[koərs]
pulse	**polsslag**	[pols·slaχ]

dizziness (vertigo)	**duiseligheid**	[dœiseliχæjt]
hot (adj)	**warm**	[varm]
shivering	**koue rillings**	[kæʊə rilliŋs]
pale (e.g., ~ face)	**bleek**	[bleək]

cough	**hoes**	[hus]
to cough (vi)	**hoes**	[hus]
to sneeze (vi)	**nies**	[nis]
faint	**floute**	[flæʊtə]
to faint (vi)	**flou word**	[flæʊ vort]

bruise (hématome)	**blou kol**	[blæʊ kol]
bump (lump)	**knop**	[knop]
to bang (bump)	**stamp**	[stamp]
contusion (bruise)	**besering**	[beseriŋ]
to limp (vi)	**hink**	[hink]
dislocation	**ontwrigting**	[ontwriχtiŋ]
to dislocate (vt)	**ontwrig**	[ontwrəχ]
fracture	**breuk**	[brøək]
to have a fracture	**n breuk hè**	[n brøək hɛ:]
cut (e.g., paper ~)	**sny**	[snaj]
to cut oneself	**jouself sny**	[jæʊsɛlf snaj]
bleeding	**bloeding**	[bludiŋ]
burn (injury)	**brandwond**	[brant·vont]
to get burned	**jouself brand**	[jæʊsɛlf brant]
to prick (vt)	**prik**	[prik]
to prick oneself	**jouself prik**	[jæʊsɛlf prik]
to injure (vt)	**seermaak**	[seərmāk]
injury	**besering**	[beseriŋ]
wound	**wond**	[vont]
trauma	**trauma**	[trɔuma]
to be delirious	**yl**	[ajl]
to stutter (vi)	**stotter**	[stottər]
sunstroke	**sonsteek**	[sɔŋ·steək]

65. Symptoms. Treatments. Part 2

pain, ache	**pyn**	[pajn]
splinter (in foot, etc.)	**splinter**	[splintər]
sweat (perspiration)	**sweet**	[sweət]
to sweat (perspire)	**sweet**	[sweət]
vomiting	**braak**	[brāk]
convulsions	**stuiptrekkings**	[stœip·trɛkkiŋs]
pregnant (adj)	**swanger**	[swaŋər]
to be born	**gebore word**	[χeborə vort]
delivery, labor	**geboorte**	[χeboərtə]
to deliver (~ a baby)	**baar**	[bār]
abortion	**aborsie**	[aborsi]
breathing, respiration	**asemhaling**	[asemhaliŋ]
in-breath (inhalation)	**inaseming**	[inasemiŋ]
out-breath (exhalation)	**uitaseming**	[œitasemiŋ]
to exhale (breathe out)	**uitasem**	[œitasem]
to inhale (vi)	**inasem**	[inasem]

disabled person	**invalide**	[infalidə]
cripple	**kreupel**	[krøəpəl]
drug addict	**dwelmslaaf**	[dwɛlm·slāf]
deaf (adj)	**doof**	[doəf]
mute (adj)	**stom**	[stom]
deaf mute (adj)	**doofstom**	[doəf·stom]
mad, insane (adj)	**swaksinnig**	[swaksinnəχ]
madman (demented person)	**kranksinnige**	[kranksinniχə]
madwoman	**kranksinnige**	[kranksinniχə]
to go insane	**kranksinnig word**	[kranksinnəχ vort]
gene	**geen**	[χeən]
immunity	**immuniteit**	[immunitæjt]
hereditary (adj)	**erflik**	[ɛrflik]
congenital (adj)	**aangebore**	[ānχəborə]
virus	**virus**	[firus]
microbe	**mikrobe**	[mikrobə]
bacterium	**bakterie**	[bakteri]
infection	**infeksie**	[infeksi]

66. Symptoms. Treatments. Part 3

hospital	**hospitaal**	[hospitāl]
patient	**pasiënt**	[pasiɛnt]
diagnosis	**diagnose**	[diaχnosə]
cure	**genesing**	[χenesiŋ]
medical treatment	**mediese behandeling**	[medisə behandəliŋ]
to get treatment	**behandeling kry**	[behandəliŋ kraj]
to treat (~ a patient)	**behandel**	[behandəl]
to nurse (look after)	**versorg**	[fersorχ]
care (nursing ~)	**versorging**	[fersorχiŋ]
operation, surgery	**operasie**	[operasi]
to bandage (head, limb)	**verbind**	[ferbint]
bandaging	**verband**	[ferbant]
vaccination	**inenting**	[inɛntiŋ]
to vaccinate (vt)	**inent**	[inɛnt]
injection, shot	**inspuiting**	[inspœitiŋ]
attack	**aanval**	[ānfal]
amputation	**amputasie**	[amputasi]
to amputate (vt)	**amputeer**	[amputeər]
coma	**koma**	[koma]
intensive care	**intensiewe sorg**	[intɛnsivə sorχ]

to recover (~ from flu)	herstel	[herstəl]
condition (patient's ~)	kondisie	[kondisi]
consciousness	bewussyn	[bevussajn]
memory (faculty)	geheue	[χəhøə]

to pull out (tooth)	trek	[trek]
filling	vulsel	[fulsəl]
to fill (a tooth)	vul	[ful]

| hypnosis | hipnose | [hipnosə] |
| to hypnotize (vt) | hipnotiseer | [hipnotiseər] |

67. Medicine. Drugs. Accessories

medicine, drug	medisyn	[medisajn]
remedy	geneesmiddel	[χeneəs·middəl]
to prescribe (vt)	voorskryf	[foərskrajf]
prescription	voorskrif	[foərskrif]

tablet, pill	pil	[pil]
ointment	salf	[salf]
ampule	ampul	[ampul]
mixture	mengsel	[meŋsəl]
syrup	stroop	[stroəp]
pill	pil	[pil]
powder	poeier	[pujer]

gauze bandage	verband	[ferbant]
cotton wool	watte	[vattə]
iodine	iodium	[iodium]

Band-Aid	pleister	[plæjstər]
eyedropper	oogdrupper	[oəχ·druppər]
thermometer	termometer	[termometər]
syringe	spuitnaald	[spœit·nālt]

| wheelchair | rolstoel | [rol·stul] |
| crutches | krukke | [krukkə] |

painkiller	pynstiller	[pajn·stillər]
laxative	lakseermiddel	[lakseər·middəl]
spirits (ethanol)	spiritus	[spiritus]
medicinal herbs	geneeskragtige kruie	[χeneəs·kraχtiχə krœiə]
herbal (~ tea)	kruie-	[krœie-]

APARTMENT

T&P Books Publishing

68. Apartment

apartment	**woonstel**	[voəŋstəl]
room	**kamer**	[kamər]
bedroom	**slaapkamer**	[slāp·kamər]
dining room	**eetkamer**	[eət·kamər]
living room	**sitkamer**	[sit·kamər]
study (home office)	**studeerkamer**	[studeər·kamər]
entry room	**ingangsportaal**	[inχaŋs·portāl]
bathroom (room with a bath or shower)	**badkamer**	[bad·kamər]
half bath	**toilet**	[tojlet]
ceiling	**plafon**	[plafon]
floor	**vloer**	[flur]
corner	**hoek**	[huk]

69. Furniture. Interior

furniture	**meubels**	[møəbɛls]
table	**tafel**	[tafel]
chair	**stoel**	[stul]
bed	**bed**	[bet]
couch, sofa	**rusbank**	[rusbank]
armchair	**gemakstoel**	[χemak·stul]
bookcase	**boekkas**	[buk·kas]
shelf	**rak**	[rak]
wardrobe	**klerekas**	[klerə·kas]
coat rack (wall-mounted ~)	**kapstok**	[kapstok]
coat stand	**kapstok**	[kapstok]
bureau, dresser	**laaikas**	[lājkas]
coffee table	**koffietafel**	[koffi·tafəl]
mirror	**spieêl**	[spiɛl]
carpet	**mat**	[mat]
rug, small carpet	**matjie**	[maki]
fireplace	**vuurherd**	[fɪr·hert]
candle	**kers**	[kers]
candlestick	**kandelaar**	[kandelār]

drapes	**gordyne**	[χordajnə]
wallpaper	**muurpapier**	[mɪr·papir]
blinds (jalousie)	**blindings**	[blindiŋs]
table lamp	**tafellamp**	[tafel·lamp]
wall lamp (sconce)	**muurlamp**	[mɪr·lamp]
floor lamp	**staanlamp**	[stān·lamp]
chandelier	**kroonlugter**	[kroən·luχtər]
leg (of chair, table)	**poot**	[poət]
armrest	**armleuning**	[arm·løəniŋ]
back (backrest)	**rugleuning**	[ruχ·løəniŋ]
drawer	**laai**	[lāi]

70. Bedding

bedclothes	**beddegoed**	[beddə·χut]
pillow	**kussing**	[kussiŋ]
pillowcase	**kussingsloop**	[kussiŋ·sloəp]
duvet, comforter	**duvet**	[dufet]
sheet	**laken**	[laken]
bedspread	**bedsprei**	[bed·spræj]

71. Kitchen

kitchen	**kombuis**	[kombœis]
gas	**gas**	[χas]
gas stove (range)	**gasstoof**	[χas·stoəf]
electric stove	**elektriese stoof**	[elektrisə stoəf]
oven	**oond**	[oent]
microwave oven	**mikrogolfoond**	[mikroχolf·oent]
refrigerator	**yskas**	[ajs·kas]
freezer	**vrieskas**	[friskas]
dishwasher	**skottelgoedwasser**	[skottelχud·wassər]
meat grinder	**vleismeul**	[flæjs·møəl]
juicer	**versapper**	[fersappər]
toaster	**broodrooster**	[broəd·roəstər]
mixer	**menger**	[meŋər]
coffee machine	**koffiemasjien**	[koffi·maʃin]
coffee pot	**koffiepot**	[koffi·pot]
coffee grinder	**koffiemeul**	[koffi·møəl]
kettle	**fluitketel**	[flœit·ketəl]
teapot	**teepot**	[teə·pot]
lid	**deksel**	[deksəl]

tea strainer	**teesiffie**	[teə·siffi]
spoon	**lepel**	[lepəl]
teaspoon	**teelepeltjie**	[teə·lepəlki]
soup spoon	**soplepel**	[sop·lepəl]
fork	**vurk**	[furk]
knife	**mes**	[mes]
tableware (dishes)	**tafelgerei**	[tafel·χeræj]
plate (dinner ~)	**bord**	[bort]
saucer	**piering**	[piriŋ]
shot glass	**likeurglas**	[likøər·χlas]
glass (tumbler)	**glas**	[χlas]
cup	**koppie**	[koppi]
sugar bowl	**suikerpot**	[sœikər·pot]
salt shaker	**soutvaatjie**	[sæʊt·fāki]
pepper shaker	**pepervaatjie**	[pepər·fāki]
butter dish	**botterbakkie**	[bottər·bakki]
stock pot (soup pot)	**soppot**	[sop·pot]
frying pan (skillet)	**braaipan**	[brāj·pan]
ladle	**opskeplepel**	[opskep·lepəl]
colander	**vergiet**	[ferχit]
tray (serving ~)	**skinkbord**	[skink·bort]
bottle	**bottel**	[bottəl]
jar (glass)	**fles**	[fles]
can	**blikkie**	[blikki]
bottle opener	**botteloopmaker**	[bottəl·oəpmakər]
can opener	**blikoopmaker**	[blik·oəpmakər]
corkscrew	**kurktrekker**	[kurk·trɛkkər]
filter	**filter**	[filtər]
to filter (vt)	**filter**	[filtər]
trash, garbage (food waste, etc.)	**vullis**	[fullis]
trash can (kitchen ~)	**vullisbak**	[fullis·bak]

72. Bathroom

bathroom	**badkamer**	[bad·kamər]
water	**water**	[vatər]
faucet	**kraan**	[krān]
hot water	**warme water**	[varmə vatər]
cold water	**koue water**	[kæʊə vatər]
toothpaste	**tandepasta**	[tandə·pasta]
to brush one's teeth	**tande borsel**	[tandə borsəl]

toothbrush	tandeborsel	[tandə·borsəl]
to shave (vi)	skeer	[skeər]
shaving foam	skeerroom	[skeər·roəm]
razor	skeermes	[skeər·mes]

to wash (one's hands, etc.)	was	[vas]
to take a bath	bad	[bat]
shower	stort	[stort]
to take a shower	stort	[stort]

bathtub	bad	[bat]
toilet (toilet bowl)	toilet	[tojlet]
sink (washbasin)	wasbak	[vas·bak]

| soap | seep | [seəp] |
| soap dish | seepbakkie | [seəp·bakki] |

sponge	spons	[spɔŋs]
shampoo	sjampoe	[ʃampu]
towel	handdoek	[handduk]
bathrobe	badjas	[batjas]

laundry (process)	was	[vas]
washing machine	wasmasjien	[vas·maʃin]
to do the laundry	die wasgoed was	[di vasχut vas]
laundry detergent	waspoeier	[vas·pujer]

73. Household appliances

TV set	TV-stel	[te·fe·stəl]
tape recorder	bandspeler	[band·spelər]
VCR (video recorder)	videomasjien	[video·maʃin]
radio	radio	[radio]
player (CD, MP3, etc.)	speler	[spelər]

video projector	videoprojektor	[video·projektor]
home movie theater	tuisfliekteater	[tœis·flik·teatər]
DVD player	DVD-speler	[de·fe·de-spelər]
amplifier	versterker	[fersterkər]
video game console	videokonsole	[video·kɔŋsolə]

video camera	videokamera	[video·kamera]
camera (photo)	kamera	[kamera]
digital camera	digitale kamera	[diχitalə kamera]

vacuum cleaner	stofsuier	[stof·sœiər]
iron (e.g., steam ~)	strykyster	[strajk·ajstər]
ironing board	strykplank	[strajk·plank]
telephone	telefoon	[telefoən]
cell phone	selfoon	[sɛlfoən]

typewriter	**tikmasjien**	[tik·maʃin]
sewing machine	**naaimasjien**	[naj·maʃin]
microphone	**mikrofoon**	[mikrofoən]
headphones	**koptelefoon**	[kop·telefoən]
remote control (TV)	**afstandsbeheer**	[afstands·beheər]
CD, compact disc	**CD**	[se·de]
cassette, tape	**kasset**	[kasset]
vinyl record	**plaat**	[plät]

THE EARTH. WEATHER

T&P Books Publishing

74. Outer space

space	**kosmos**	[kosmos]
space (as adj)	**kosmies**	[kosmis]
outer space	**buitenste ruimte**	[bœitɛŋstə rajmtə]
world	**wêreld**	[værɛlt]
universe	**heelal**	[heəlal]
galaxy	**sterrestelsel**	[sterrə·stɛlsəl]
star	**ster**	[ster]
constellation	**sterrebeeld**	[sterrə·beəlt]
planet	**planeet**	[planeət]
satellite	**satelliet**	[satɛllit]
meteorite	**meteoriet**	[meteorit]
comet	**komeet**	[komeət]
asteroid	**asteroïed**	[asteroïət]
orbit	**baan**	[bãn]
to revolve	**draai**	[drãi]
(~ around the Earth)		
atmosphere	**atmosfeer**	[atmosfeər]
the Sun	**die Son**	[di son]
solar system	**sonnestelsel**	[sonnə·stɛlsəl]
solar eclipse	**sonsverduistering**	[soŋs·ferdœisteriŋ]
the Earth	**die Aarde**	[di ãrdə]
the Moon	**die Maan**	[di mãn]
Mars	**Mars**	[mars]
Venus	**Venus**	[fenus]
Jupiter	**Jupiter**	[jupitər]
Saturn	**Saturnus**	[saturnus]
Mercury	**Mercurius**	[merkurius]
Uranus	**Uranus**	[uranus]
Neptune	**Neptunus**	[neptunus]
Pluto	**Pluto**	[pluto]
Milky Way	**Melkweg**	[melk·weχ]
Great Bear (Ursa Major)	**Groot Beer**	[χroət beər]
North Star	**Poolster**	[poəl·stər]
Martian	**marsbewoner**	[mars·bevonər]
extraterrestrial (n)	**buiteaardse wese**	[bœitə·ãrdsə vesə]

alien	ruimtewese	[rœimtə·vesə]
flying saucer	vlieënde skottel	[fliɛndə skottəl]
spaceship	ruimteskip	[rœimtə·skip]
space station	ruimtestasie	[rœimtə·stasi]
blast-off	vertrek	[fertrek]
engine	enjin	[ɛndʒin]
nozzle	uitlaatpyp	[œitlāt·pajp]
fuel	brandstof	[brantstof]
cockpit, flight deck	stuurkajuit	[stɪr·kajœit]
antenna	lugdraad	[luχdrāt]
porthole	patryspoort	[patrajs·poərt]
solar panel	sonpaneel	[son·paneəl]
spacesuit	ruimtepak	[rœimtə·pak]
weightlessness	gewigloosheid	[χeviχloəshæjt]
oxygen	suurstof	[sɪrstof]
docking (in space)	koppeling	[koppeliŋ]
to dock (vi, vt)	koppel	[koppəl]
observatory	observatorium	[observatorium]
telescope	teleskoop	[teleskoəp]
to observe (vt)	waarneem	[vārneəm]
to explore (vt)	eksploreer	[ɛksploreər]

75. The Earth

the Earth	die Aarde	[di ārdə]
the globe (the Earth)	die aardbol	[di ārdbol]
planet	planeet	[planeət]
atmosphere	atmosfeer	[atmosfeər]
geography	geografie	[χeoχrafi]
nature	natuur	[natɪr]
globe (table ~)	aardbol	[ārd·bol]
map	kaart	[kārt]
atlas	atlas	[atlas]
Europe	Europa	[øəropa]
Asia	Asië	[asiɛ]
Africa	Afrika	[afrika]
Australia	Australië	[oustraliɛ]
America	Amerika	[amerika]
North America	Noord-Amerika	[noərd-amerika]
South America	Suid-Amerika	[sœid-amerika]

| Antarctica | **Suidpool** | [sœid·poəl] |
| the Arctic | **Noordpool** | [noərd·poəl] |

76. Cardinal directions

north	**noorde**	[noərdə]
to the north	**na die noorde**	[na di noərdə]
in the north	**in die noorde**	[in di noərdə]
northern (adj)	**noordelik**	[noərdəlik]
south	**suide**	[sœidə]
to the south	**na die suide**	[na di sœidə]
in the south	**in die suide**	[in di sœidə]
southern (adj)	**suidelik**	[sœidəlik]
west	**weste**	[vestə]
to the west	**na die weste**	[na di vestə]
in the west	**in die weste**	[in di vestə]
western (adj)	**westelik**	[vestelik]
east	**ooste**	[oəstə]
to the east	**na die ooste**	[na di oəstə]
in the east	**in die ooste**	[in di oəstə]
eastern (adj)	**oostelik**	[oəstəlik]

77. Sea. Ocean

sea	**see**	[seə]
ocean	**oseaan**	[oseãn]
gulf (bay)	**golf**	[χolf]
straits	**straat**	[strãt]
land (solid ground)	**land**	[lant]
continent (mainland)	**kontinent**	[kontinent]
island	**eiland**	[æjlant]
peninsula	**skiereiland**	[skir·æjlant]
archipelago	**argipel**	[arχipəl]
bay, cove	**baai**	[bãi]
harbor	**hawe**	[havə]
lagoon	**strandmeer**	[strand·meər]
cape	**kaap**	[kãp]
atoll	**atol**	[atol]
reef	**rif**	[rif]
coral	**koraal**	[korãl]
coral reef	**koraalrif**	[korãl·rif]

deep (adj)	**diep**	[dip]
depth (deep water)	**diepte**	[diptə]
abyss	**afgrond**	[afχront]
trench (e.g., Mariana ~)	**trog**	[troχ]
current (Ocean ~)	**stroming**	[stromiŋ]
to surround (bathe)	**omring**	[omriŋ]
shore	**oewer**	[uvər]
coast	**kus**	[kus]
flow (flood tide)	**hoogwater**	[hoəχ·vatər]
ebb (ebb tide)	**laagwater**	[lāχ·vatər]
shoal	**sandbank**	[sand·bank]
bottom (~ of the sea)	**bodem**	[bodem]
wave	**golf**	[χolf]
crest (~ of a wave)	**kruin**	[krœin]
spume (sea foam)	**skuim**	[skœim]
storm (sea storm)	**storm**	[storm]
hurricane	**orkaan**	[orkān]
tsunami	**tsunami**	[tsunami]
calm (dead ~)	**windstilte**	[vindstiltə]
quiet, calm (adj)	**kalm**	[kalm]
pole	**pool**	[poəl]
polar (adj)	**polêr**	[polær]
latitude	**breedtegraad**	[breədtə·χrāt]
longitude	**lengtegraad**	[leŋtə·χrāt]
parallel	**parallel**	[paralləl]
equator	**ewenaar**	[ɛvenār]
sky	**hemel**	[heməl]
horizon	**horison**	[horison]
air	**lug**	[luχ]
lighthouse	**vuurtoring**	[fɪrtoriŋ]
to dive (vi)	**duik**	[dœik]
to sink (ab. boat)	**sink**	[sink]
treasures	**skatte**	[skattə]

78. Seas' and Oceans' names

Atlantic Ocean	**Atlantiese oseaan**	[atlantisə oseān]
Indian Ocean	**Indiese Oseaan**	[indisə oseān]
Pacific Ocean	**Stille Oseaan**	[stillə oseān]
Arctic Ocean	**Noordelike Yssee**	[noərdelikə ajs·seə]
Black Sea	**Swart See**	[swart seə]

Red Sea	**Rooi See**	[roj seə]
Yellow Sea	**Geel See**	[χeəl seə]
White Sea	**Witsee**	[vit·seə]

Caspian Sea	**Kaspiese See**	[kaspisə seə]
Dead Sea	**Dooie See**	[doje seə]
Mediterranean Sea	**Middellandse See**	[middəllandsə seə]

| Aegean Sea | **Egeïese See** | [εχejesə seə] |
| Adriatic Sea | **Adriatiese See** | [adriatisə seə] |

Arabian Sea	**Arabiese See**	[arabisə seə]
Sea of Japan	**Japanse See**	[japaŋsə seə]
Bering Sea	**Beringsee**	[beriŋ·seə]
South China Sea	**Suid-Sjinese See**	[sœid-ʃinesə seə]

Coral Sea	**Koraalsee**	[korāl·seə]
Tasman Sea	**Tasmansee**	[tasmaŋ·seə]
Caribbean Sea	**Karibiese See**	[karibisə seə]

| Barents Sea | **Barentssee** | [barents·seə] |
| Kara Sea | **Karasee** | [kara·seə] |

North Sea	**Noordsee**	[noərd·seə]
Baltic Sea	**Baltiese See**	[baltisə seə]
Norwegian Sea	**Noorse See**	[noərsə seə]

79. Mountains

mountain	**berg**	[berχ]
mountain range	**bergreeks**	[berχ·reəks]
mountain ridge	**bergrug**	[berχ·ruχ]

summit, top	**top**	[top]
peak	**piek**	[pik]
foot (~ of the mountain)	**voet**	[fut]
slope (mountainside)	**helling**	[hεlliŋ]

volcano	**vulkaan**	[fulkān]
active volcano	**aktiewe vulkaan**	[aktivə fulkān]
dormant volcano	**rustende vulkaan**	[rustendə fulkān]

eruption	**uitbarsting**	[œitbarstiŋ]
crater	**krater**	[kratər]
magma	**magma**	[maχma]
lava	**lawa**	[lava]
molten (~ lava)	**gloeiende**	[χlujendə]

| canyon | **diepkloof** | [dip·kloəf] |
| gorge | **kloof** | [kloəf] |

crevice	**skeur**	[skøər]
abyss (chasm)	**afgrond**	[afχront]
pass, col	**bergpas**	[berχ·pas]
plateau	**plato**	[plato]
cliff	**krans**	[kraŋs]
hill	**kop**	[kop]
glacier	**gletser**	[χletsər]
waterfall	**waterval**	[vatər·fal]
geyser	**geiser**	[χæjsər]
lake	**meer**	[meər]
plain	**vlakte**	[flaktə]
landscape	**landskap**	[landskap]
echo	**eggo**	[εχχo]
alpinist	**alpinis**	[alpinis]
rock climber	**bergklimmer**	[berχ·klimmər]
to conquer (in climbing)	**baasraak**	[bāsrāk]
climb (an easy ~)	**beklimming**	[beklimmiŋ]

80. Mountains names

The Alps	**die Alpe**	[di alpə]
Mont Blanc	**Mont Blanc**	[mon blan]
The Pyrenees	**die Pireneë**	[di pireneε]
The Carpathians	**die Karpate**	[di karpatə]
The Ural Mountains	**die Oeralgebergte**	[di ural·χəberχtə]
The Caucasus Mountains	**die Koukasus Gebergte**	[di kæʊkasus χəberχtə]
Mount Elbrus	**Elbroes**	[εlbrus]
The Altai Mountains	**die Altai-gebergte**	[di altaj·χəberχtə]
The Tian Shan	**die Tian Shan**	[di tian ʃan]
The Pamir Mountains	**die Pamir**	[di pamir]
The Himalayas	**die Himalajas**	[di himalajas]
Mount Everest	**Everest**	[εverest]
The Andes	**die Andes**	[di andes]
Mount Kilimanjaro	**Kilimanjaro**	[kilimandʒaro]

81. Rivers

river	**rivier**	[rifir]
spring (natural source)	**bron**	[bron]
riverbed (river channel)	**rivierbed**	[rifir·bet]
basin (river valley)	**stroomgebied**	[stroəm·χebit]

to flow into …	uitmond in …	[œitmont in …]
tributary	syrivier	[saj·rifir]
bank (of river)	oewer	[uvər]

current (stream)	stroming	[stromiŋ]
downstream (adv)	stroomafwaarts	[stroəm·afvārts]
upstream (adv)	stroomopwaarts	[stroəm·opvārts]

inundation	oorstroming	[oərstromiŋ]
flooding	oorstroming	[oərstromiŋ]
to overflow (vi)	oor sy walle loop	[oər saj vallə loəp]
to flood (vt)	oorstroom	[oərstroəm]

| shallow (shoal) | sandbank | [sand·bank] |
| rapids | stroomversnellings | [stroəm·fersnɛlliŋs] |

dam	damwal	[dam·wal]
canal	kanaal	[kanāl]
reservoir (artificial lake)	opgaardam	[opχār·dam]
sluice, lock	sluis	[slœis]

water body (pond, etc.)	dam	[dam]
swamp (marshland)	moeras	[muras]
bog, marsh	vlei	[flæj]
whirlpool	draaikolk	[drāj·kolk]

stream (brook)	spruit	[sprœit]
drinking (ab. water)	drink-	[drink-]
fresh (~ water)	vars	[fars]

ice	ys	[ajs]
to freeze over	bevries	[befris]
(ab. river, etc.)		

82. Rivers' names

| Seine | Seine | [sæjn] |
| Loire | Loire | [lua:r] |

Thames	Teems	[tems]
Rhine	Ryn	[rajn]
Danube	Donau	[donɔu]

Volga	Wolga	[volga]
Don	Don	[don]
Lena	Lena	[lena]

Yellow River	Geel Rivier	[χeəl rifir]
Yangtze	Blou Rivier	[blæʊ rifir]
Mekong	Mekong	[mekoŋ]

Ganges	**Ganges**	[xaŋəs]
Nile River	**Nyl**	[najl]
Congo River	**Kongorivier**	[kongo·rifir]
Okavango River	**Okavango**	[okavaŋgo]
Zambezi River	**Zambezi**	[sambesi]
Limpopo River	**Limpopo**	[limpopo]
Mississippi River	**Mississippi**	[mississippi]

83. Forest

forest, wood	**bos**	[bos]
forest (as adj)	**bos-**	[bos-]
thick forest	**woud**	[væʊt]
grove	**boord**	[boərt]
forest clearing	**oopte**	[oəptə]
thicket	**struikgewas**	[strœik·xevas]
scrubland	**struikveld**	[strœik·fɛlt]
footpath (troddenpath)	**paadjie**	[pādʒi]
gully	**donga**	[donxa]
tree	**boom**	[boəm]
leaf	**blaar**	[blār]
leaves (foliage)	**blare**	[blarə]
fall of leaves	**val van die blare**	[fal fan di blarə]
to fall (ab. leaves)	**val**	[fal]
top (of the tree)	**boomtop**	[boəm·top]
branch	**tak**	[tak]
bough	**tak**	[tak]
bud (on shrub, tree)	**knop**	[knop]
needle (of pine tree)	**naald**	[nālt]
pine cone	**dennebol**	[dɛnnə·bol]
hollow (in a tree)	**holte**	[holtə]
nest	**nes**	[nes]
burrow (animal hole)	**gat**	[xat]
trunk	**stam**	[stam]
root	**wortel**	[vortəl]
bark	**bas**	[bas]
moss	**mos**	[mos]
to uproot (remove trees or tree stumps)	**ontwortel**	[ontwortəl]
to chop down	**omkap**	[omkap]
to deforest (vt)	**ontbos**	[ontbos]

tree stump	**boomstomp**	[boəm·stomp]
campfire	**kampvuur**	[kampfɪr]
forest fire	**bosbrand**	[bos·brant]
to extinguish (vt)	**blus**	[blus]

forest ranger	**boswagter**	[bos·waχtər]
protection	**beskerming**	[beskermiŋ]
to protect (~ nature)	**beskerm**	[beskerm]
poacher	**wildstroper**	[vilt·stropər]
steel trap	**slagyster**	[slaχ·ajstər]

| to gather, to pick (vt) | **pluk** | [pluk] |
| to lose one's way | **verdwaal** | [ferdwāl] |

84. Natural resources

natural resources	**natuurlike bronne**	[natɪrlikə bronnə]
minerals	**minerale**	[mineralə]
deposits	**lae**	[laə]
field (e.g., oilfield)	**veld**	[fɛlt]

to mine (extract)	**myn**	[majn]
mining (extraction)	**myn**	[majn]
ore	**erts**	[ɛrts]
mine (e.g., for coal)	**myn**	[majn]
shaft (mine ~)	**mynskag**	[majn·skaχ]
miner	**mynwerker**	[majn·werkər]

| gas (natural ~) | **gas** | [χas] |
| gas pipeline | **gaspyp** | [χas·pajp] |

oil (petroleum)	**olie**	[oli]
oil pipeline	**olipypleiding**	[oli·pajp·læjdiŋ]
oil well	**oliebron**	[oli·bron]
derrick (tower)	**boortoring**	[boər·toriŋ]
tanker	**tenkskip**	[tɛnk·skip]

sand	**sand**	[sant]
limestone	**kalksteen**	[kalksteən]
gravel	**gruis**	[χrœis]
peat	**veengrond**	[feənχront]
clay	**klei**	[klæj]
coal	**steenkool**	[steən·koəl]

iron (ore)	**yster**	[ajstər]
gold	**goud**	[χæʊt]
silver	**silwer**	[silwər]
nickel	**nikkel**	[nikkəl]
copper	**koper**	[kopər]
zinc	**sink**	[sink]

manganese	mangaan	[manχān]
mercury	kwik	[kwik]
lead	lood	[loət]
mineral	mineraal	[minerāl]
crystal	kristal	[kristal]
marble	marmer	[marmər]
uranium	uraan	[urān]

85. Weather

weather	weer	[veər]
weather forecast	weersvoorspelling	[veərs·foərspɛllɪŋ]
temperature	temperatuur	[temperatɪr]
thermometer	termometer	[termometər]
barometer	barometer	[barometər]
humid (adj)	klam	[klam]
humidity	vogtigheid	[foχtiχæjt]
heat (extreme ~)	hitte	[hittə]
hot (torrid)	heet	[heət]
it's hot	dis vrekwarm	[dis frekvarm]
it's warm	dit is warm	[dit is varm]
warm (moderately hot)	louwarm	[læʊvarm]
it's cold	dis koud	[dis kæʊt]
cold (adj)	koud	[kæʊt]
sun	son	[son]
to shine (vi)	skyn	[skajn]
sunny (day)	sonnig	[sonnəχ]
to come up (vi)	opkom	[opkom]
to set (vi)	ondergaan	[ondərχān]
cloud	wolk	[volk]
cloudy (adj)	bewolk	[bevolk]
rain cloud	reënwolk	[reɛn·wolk]
somber (gloomy)	somber	[sombər]
rain	reën	[reɛn]
it's raining	dit reën	[dit reɛn]
rainy (~ day, weather)	reënerig	[reɛnerəχ]
to drizzle (vi)	motreën	[motreɛn]
pouring rain	stortbui	[stortbœi]
downpour	reënvlaag	[reɛn·flāχ]
heavy (e.g., ~ rain)	swaar	[swār]
puddle	poeletjie	[puləki]

to get wet (in rain)	nat word	[nat vort]
fog (mist)	mis	[mis]
foggy	mistig	[mistəχ]
snow	sneeu	[sniʊ]
it's snowing	dit sneeu	[dit sniʊ]

86. Severe weather. Natural disasters

thunderstorm	donderstorm	[dondər·storm]
lightning (~ strike)	weerlig	[veərləχ]
to flash (vi)	flits	[flits]
thunder	donder	[dondər]
to thunder (vi)	donder	[dondər]
it's thundering	dit donder	[dit dondər]
hail	hael	[haəl]
it's hailing	dit hael	[dit haəl]
to flood (vt)	oorstroom	[oərstroəm]
flood, inundation	oorstroming	[oərstrominŋ]
earthquake	aardbewing	[ārd·bevinŋ]
tremor, quake	aardskok	[ārd·skok]
epicenter	episentrum	[ɛpisentrum]
eruption	uitbarsting	[œitbarstinŋ]
lava	lawa	[lava]
twister, tornado	tornado	[tornado]
typhoon	tifoon	[tifoən]
hurricane	orkaan	[orkān]
storm	storm	[storm]
tsunami	tsunami	[tsunami]
cyclone	sikloon	[sikloən]
bad weather	slegte weer	[sleχtə veər]
fire (accident)	brand	[brant]
disaster	ramp	[ramp]
meteorite	meteoriet	[meteorit]
avalanche	lawine	[lavinə]
snowslide	sneeulawine	[sniʊ·lavinə]
blizzard	sneeustorm	[sniʊ·storm]
snowstorm	sneeustorm	[sniʊ·storm]

FAUNA

T&P Books Publishing

87. Mammals. Predators

predator	**roofdier**	[roəf·dir]
tiger	**tier**	[tir]
lion	**leeu**	[liʊ]
wolf	**wolf**	[volf]
fox	**vos**	[fos]
jaguar	**jaguar**	[jaχuar]
leopard	**luiperd**	[lœipert]
cheetah	**jagluiperd**	[jaχ·lœipert]
black panther	**swart luiperd**	[swart lœipert]
puma	**poema**	[puma]
snow leopard	**sneeuluiperd**	[sniʊ·lœipert]
lynx	**los**	[los]
coyote	**prèriewolf**	[præri·volf]
jackal	**jakkals**	[jakkals]
hyena	**hiëna**	[hiɛna]

88. Wild animals

animal	**dier**	[dir]
beast (animal)	**beest**	[beəst]
squirrel	**eekhoring**	[eəkhoriŋ]
hedgehog	**krimpvarkie**	[krimpfarki]
hare	**hasie**	[hasi]
rabbit	**konyn**	[konajn]
badger	**das**	[das]
raccoon	**wasbeer**	[vasbeər]
hamster	**hamster**	[hamstər]
marmot	**marmot**	[marmot]
mole	**mol**	[mol]
mouse	**muis**	[mœis]
rat	**rot**	[rot]
bat	**vlermuis**	[fler·mœis]
ermine	**hermelyn**	[herməlajn]
sable	**sabel, sabeldier**	[sabəl], [sabəl·dir]
marten	**marter**	[martər]

weasel	**wesel**	[vesəl]
mink	**nerts**	[nerts]
beaver	**bewer**	[bevər]
otter	**otter**	[ottər]
horse	**perd**	[pert]
moose	**eland**	[ɛlant]
deer	**hert**	[hert]
camel	**kameel**	[kameəl]
bison	**bison**	[bison]
aurochs	**wisent**	[visent]
buffalo	**buffel**	[buffəl]
zebra	**sebra, kwagga**	[sebra], [kwaχχa]
antelope	**wildsbok**	[vilds·bok]
roe deer	**reebok**	[reəbok]
fallow deer	**damhert**	[damhert]
chamois	**gems**	[χems]
wild boar	**wildevark**	[vildə·fark]
whale	**walvis**	[valfis]
seal	**seehond**	[seə·hont]
walrus	**walrus**	[valrus]
fur seal	**seebeer**	[seə·beər]
dolphin	**dolfyn**	[dolfajn]
bear	**beer**	[beər]
polar bear	**ysbeer**	[ajs·beər]
panda	**panda**	[panda]
monkey	**aap**	[āp]
chimpanzee	**sjimpansee**	[ʃimpaŋseə]
orangutan	**orangoetang**	[oranχutaŋ]
gorilla	**gorilla**	[χorilla]
macaque	**makaak**	[makāk]
gibbon	**gibbon**	[χibbon]
elephant	**olifant**	[olifant]
rhinoceros	**renoster**	[renostər]
giraffe	**kameelperd**	[kameəl·pert]
hippopotamus	**seekoei**	[seə·kui]
kangaroo	**kangaroe**	[kanχaru]
koala (bear)	**koala**	[koala]
mongoose	**muishond**	[mœis·hont]
chinchilla	**chinchilla, tjintjilla**	[tʃin·tʃila]
skunk	**stinkmuishond**	[stinkmœis·hont]
porcupine	**ystervark**	[ajstər·fark]

89. Domestic animals

cat	kat	[kat]
tomcat	kater	[katər]
dog	hond	[hont]

horse	perd	[pert]
stallion (male horse)	hings	[hiŋs]
mare	merrie	[merri]

cow	koei	[kui]
bull	bul	[bul]
ox	os	[os]

sheep (ewe)	skaap	[skāp]
ram	ram	[ram]
goat	bok	[bok]
billy goat, he-goat	bokram	[bok·ram]

| donkey | donkie, esel | [donki], [eisəl] |
| mule | muil | [mœil] |

pig, hog	vark	[fark]
piglet	varkie	[farki]
rabbit	konyn	[konajn]

| hen (chicken) | hoender, hen | [hundər], [hen] |
| rooster | haan | [hān] |

duck	eend	[eent]
drake	mannetjieseend	[mannəkis·eent]
goose	gans	[χaŋs]

| tom turkey, gobbler | kalkoenmannetjie | [kalkun·mannəki] |
| turkey (hen) | kalkoen | [kalkun] |

domestic animals	huisdiere	[hœis·dirə]
tame (e.g., ~ hamster)	mak	[mak]
to tame (vt)	mak maak	[mak māk]
to breed (vt)	teel	[teəl]

farm	plaas	[plās]
poultry	pluimvee	[plœimfeə]
cattle	beeste	[beəstə]
herd (cattle)	kudde	[kuddə]

stable	stal	[stal]
pigpen	varkstal	[fark·stal]
cowshed	koeistal	[kui·stal]
rabbit hutch	konynehok	[konajnə·hok]
hen house	hoenderhok	[hundər·hok]

90. Birds

bird	voël	[foɛl]
pigeon	duif	[dœif]
sparrow	mossie	[mossi]
tit (great tit)	mees	[meəs]
magpie	ekster	[ɛkstər]
raven	raaf	[rãf]
crow	kraai	[krãi]
jackdaw	kerkkraai	[kerk·krãi]
rook	roek	[ruk]
duck	eend	[eent]
goose	gans	[χaŋs]
pheasant	fisant	[fisant]
eagle	arend	[arɛnt]
hawk	sperwer	[sperwər]
falcon	valk	[falk]
vulture	aasvoël	[ãsfoɛl]
condor (Andean ~)	kondor	[kondor]
swan	swaan	[swãn]
crane	kraanvoël	[krãn·foɛl]
stork	ooievaar	[ojefãr]
parrot	papegaai	[papəχãi]
hummingbird	kolibrie	[kolibri]
peacock	pou	[pæʊ]
ostrich	volstruis	[folstrœis]
heron	reier	[ræjer]
flamingo	flamink	[flamink]
pelican	pelikaan	[pelikãn]
nightingale	nagtegaal	[naχteχãl]
swallow	swael	[swaəl]
thrush	lyster	[lajstər]
song thrush	sanglyster	[saŋlajstər]
blackbird	merel	[merəl]
swift	windswael	[vindswaəl]
lark	lewerik	[leverik]
quail	kwartel	[kwartəl]
woodpecker	speg	[speχ]
cuckoo	koekoek	[kukuk]
owl	uil	[œil]
eagle owl	ooruil	[oərœil]

wood grouse	**auerhoen**	[ɔuer·hun]
black grouse	**korhoen**	[korhun]
partridge	**patrys**	[patrajs]
starling	**spreeu**	[spriʊ]
canary	**kanarie**	[kanari]
hazel grouse	**bonasa hoen**	[bonasa hun]
chaffinch	**gryskoppie**	[ɣrajskoppi]
bullfinch	**bloedvink**	[bludfink]
seagull	**seemeeu**	[seəmiʊ]
albatross	**albatros**	[albatros]
penguin	**pikkewyn**	[pikkəvajn]

91. Fish. Marine animals

bream	**brasem**	[brasem]
carp	**karp**	[karp]
perch	**baars**	[bārs]
catfish	**katvis, seebaber**	[katfis], [seə·babər]
pike	**snoek**	[snuk]
salmon	**salm**	[salm]
sturgeon	**steur**	[støər]
herring	**haring**	[hariŋ]
Atlantic salmon	**atlantiese salm**	[atlantisə salm]
mackerel	**makriel**	[makril]
flatfish	**platvis**	[platfis]
zander, pike perch	**varswatersnoek**	[farswatər·snuk]
cod	**kabeljou**	[kabeljæʊ]
tuna	**tuna**	[tuna]
trout	**forel**	[forəl]
eel	**paling**	[paliŋ]
electric ray	**drilvis**	[drilfis]
moray eel	**bontpaling**	[bontpaliŋ]
piranha	**piranha**	[piranha]
shark	**haai**	[hāi]
dolphin	**dolfyn**	[dolfajn]
whale	**walvis**	[valfis]
crab	**krap**	[krap]
jellyfish	**jellievis**	[jelli·fis]
octopus	**seekat**	[seə·kat]
starfish	**seester**	[seə·stər]
sea urchin	**see-egel, seekastaiing**	[seə-eɣel], [seə·kastajiŋ]

seahorse	seeperdjie	[seə·perdʒi]
oyster	oester	[ustər]
shrimp	garnaal	[χarnãl]
lobster	kreef	[kreəf]
spiny lobster	seekreef	[seə·kreəf]

92. Amphibians. Reptiles

snake	slang	[slaŋ]
venomous (snake)	giftig	[χiftəχ]
viper	adder	[addər]
cobra	kobra	[kobra]
python	luislang	[lœislaŋ]
boa	boa, konstriktorslang	[boa], [kɔŋstriktor·slaŋ]
grass snake	ringslang	[riŋ·slaŋ]
rattle snake	ratelslang	[ratəl·slaŋ]
anaconda	anakonda	[anakonda]
lizard	akkedis	[akkedis]
iguana	leguaan	[leχuãn]
monitor lizard	likkewaan	[likkevãn]
salamander	salamander	[salamandər]
chameleon	verkleurmannetjie	[ferkløər·manneki]
scorpion	skerpioen	[skerpiun]
turtle	skilpad	[skilpat]
frog	padda	[padda]
toad	brulpadda	[brul·padda]
crocodile	krokodil	[krokodil]

93. Insects

insect, bug	insek	[insek]
butterfly	skoenlapper	[skunlappər]
ant	mier	[mir]
fly	vlieg	[fliχ]
mosquito	muskiet	[muskit]
beetle	kewer	[kevər]
wasp	perdeby	[perdə·baj]
bee	by	[baj]
bumblebee	hommelby	[homməl·baj]
gadfly (botfly)	perdevlieg	[perdə·fliχ]
spider	spinnekop	[spinnə·kop]
spiderweb	spinnerak	[spinnə·rak]

dragonfly	naaldekoker	[nāldə·kokər]
grasshopper	sprinkaan	[sprinkān]
moth (night butterfly)	mot	[mot]

cockroach	kakkerlak	[kakkerlak]
tick	bosluis	[boslœis]
flea	vlooi	[floj]
midge	muggie	[muχχi]

locust	treksprinkhaan	[trek·sprinkhān]
snail	slak	[slak]
cricket	kriek	[krik]
lightning bug	vuurvliegie	[fɪrfliχi]
ladybug	lieweheersbesie	[liveheərs·besi]
cockchafer	lentekewer	[lentekevər]

leech	bloedsuier	[blud·sœiər]
caterpillar	ruspe	[ruspə]
earthworm	erdwurm	[ɛrd·vurm]
larva	larwe	[larvə]

FLORA

T&P Books Publishing

tree	**boom**	[boəm]
deciduous (adj)	**bladwisselend**	[bladwisselent]
coniferous (adj)	**kegeldraend**	[keχɛldraent]
evergreen (adj)	**immergroen**	[immərχrun]
apple tree	**appelboom**	[appɛl·boəm]
pear tree	**peerboom**	[peər·boəm]
cherry tree	**kersieboom**	[kersi·boəm]
sweet cherry tree	**soetkersieboom**	[sutkersi·boəm]
sour cherry tree	**suurkersieboom**	[sɪrkersi·boəm]
plum tree	**pruimeboom**	[prœimə·boəm]
birch	**berk**	[berk]
oak	**eik**	[æjk]
linden tree	**lindeboom**	[lində·boəm]
aspen	**trilpopulier**	[trilpopulir]
maple	**esdoring**	[ɛsdoriŋ]
spruce	**spar**	[spar]
pine	**denneboom**	[dɛnnə·boəm]
larch	**lorkeboom**	[lorkə·boəm]
fir tree	**den**	[den]
cedar	**seder**	[sedər]
poplar	**populier**	[populir]
rowan	**lysterbessie**	[lajstərbɛssi]
willow	**wilger**	[vilχər]
alder	**els**	[ɛls]
beech	**beuk**	[bøək]
elm	**olm**	[olm]
ash (tree)	**esboom**	[ɛs·boəm]
chestnut	**kastaiing**	[kastajiŋ]
magnolia	**magnolia**	[maχnolia]
palm tree	**palm**	[palm]
cypress	**sipres**	[sipres]
mangrove	**wortelboom**	[vortəl·boəm]
baobab	**kremetart**	[kremetart]
eucalyptus	**bloekom**	[blukom]
sequoia	**mammoetboom**	[mammut·boəm]

95. Shrubs

bush	struik	[strœik]
shrub	bossie	[bossi]
grapevine	wingerdstok	[viŋərd·stok]
vineyard	wingerd	[viŋərt]
raspberry bush	framboosstruik	[framboəs·strœik]
blackcurrant bush	swartbessiestruik	[swartbɛssi·strœik]
redcurrant bush	rooi aalbessiestruik	[roj ālbɛssi·strœik]
gooseberry bush	appelliefiestruik	[appɛllifi·strœik]
acacia	akasia	[akasia]
barberry	suurbessie	[sɪr·bɛssi]
jasmine	jasmyn	[jasmajn]
juniper	jenewer	[jenevər]
rosebush	roosstruik	[roəs·strœik]
dog rose	hondsroos	[honds·roəs]

96. Fruits. Berries

fruit	vrug	[fruχ]
fruits	vrugte	[fruχtə]
apple	appel	[appəl]
pear	peer	[peər]
plum	pruim	[prœim]
strawberry (garden ~)	aarbei	[ārbæj]
cherry	kersie	[kersi]
sour cherry	suurkersie	[sɪr·kersi]
sweet cherry	soetkersie	[sut·kersi]
grape	druif	[drœif]
raspberry	framboos	[framboəs]
blackcurrant	swartbessie	[swartbɛssi]
redcurrant	rooi aalbessie	[roj ālbɛssi]
gooseberry	appelliefie	[appɛllifi]
cranberry	bosbessie	[bosbɛssi]
orange	lemoen	[lemun]
mandarin	nartjie	[narki]
pineapple	pynappel	[pajnappəl]
banana	piesang	[pisaŋ]
date	dadel	[dadəl]
lemon	suurlemoen	[sɪr·lemun]
apricot	appelkoos	[appɛlkoəs]

peach	perske	[perskə]
kiwi	kiwi, kiwivrug	[kivi], [kivi·fruχ]
grapefruit	pomelo	[pomelo]

berry	bessie	[bɛssi]
berries	bessies	[bɛssis]
cowberry	pryselbessie	[prajsɛlbɛssi]
wild strawberry	wilde aarbei	[vildə ārbæj]
bilberry	bloubessie	[blæʊbɛssi]

97. Flowers. Plants

flower	blom	[blom]
bouquet (of flowers)	boeket	[buket]

rose (flower)	roos	[roəs]
tulip	tulp	[tulp]
carnation	angelier	[anχəlir]
gladiolus	swaardlelie	[swārd·leli]

cornflower	koringblom	[koriŋblom]
harebell	grasklokkie	[χras·klokki]
dandelion	perdeblom	[perdə·blom]
camomile	kamille	[kamillə]

aloe	aalwyn	[ālwajn]
cactus	kaktus	[kaktus]
rubber plant, ficus	rubberplant	[rubbər·plant]

lily	lelie	[leli]
geranium	malva	[malfa]
hyacinth	hiasint	[hiasint]

mimosa	mimosa	[mimosa]
narcissus	narsing	[narsiŋ]
nasturtium	kappertjie	[kapperki]

orchid	orgidee	[orχideə]
peony	pinksterroos	[pinkstər·roəs]
violet	viooltjie	[fioəlki]

pansy	gesiggie	[χesiχi]
forget-me-not	vergeet-my-nietjie	[ferχeət-maj-niki]
daisy	madeliefie	[madelifi]

poppy	papawer	[papavər]
hemp	hennep	[hɛnnəp]
mint	kruisement	[krœisəment]
lily of the valley	dallelie	[dalleli]
snowdrop	sneeuklokkie	[sniʊ·klokki]

nettle	**brandnetel**	[brant·netəl]
sorrel	**veldsuring**	[fɛltsuriŋ]
water lily	**waterlelie**	[vatər·leli]
fern	**varing**	[fariŋ]
lichen	**korsmos**	[korsmos]
greenhouse (tropical ~)	**broeikas**	[bruikas]
lawn	**grasperk**	[xras·perk]
flowerbed	**blombed**	[blom·bet]
plant	**plant**	[plant]
grass	**gras**	[xras]
blade of grass	**grasspriet**	[xras·sprit]
leaf	**blaar**	[blār]
petal	**kroonblaar**	[kroən·blār]
stem	**stingel**	[stiŋəl]
tuber	**knol**	[knol]
young plant (shoot)	**saailing**	[sājliŋ]
thorn	**doring**	[doriŋ]
to blossom (vi)	**bloei**	[blui]
to fade, to wither	**verlep**	[ferlep]
smell (odor)	**reuk**	[røək]
to cut (flowers)	**sny**	[snaj]
to pick (a flower)	**pluk**	[pluk]

98. Cereals, grains

grain	**graan**	[xrān]
cereal crops	**graangewasse**	[xrān·xəwassə]
ear (of barley, etc.)	**aar**	[ār]
wheat	**koring**	[koriŋ]
rye	**rog**	[roχ]
oats	**hawer**	[havər]
millet	**gierst**	[xirst]
barley	**gars**	[xars]
corn	**mielie**	[mili]
rice	**rys**	[rajs]
buckwheat	**bokwiet**	[bokwit]
pea plant	**ertjie**	[ɛrki]
kidney bean	**nierboon**	[nir·boən]
soy	**soja**	[soja]
lentil	**lensie**	[lɛŋsi]
beans (pulse crops)	**boontjies**	[boənkis]

COUNTRIES OF
THE WORLD

T&P Books Publishing

Afghanistan	**Afghanistan**	[afχanistan]
Albania	**Albanië**	[albaniɛ]
Argentina	**Argentinië**	[arχentiniɛ]
Armenia	**Armenië**	[armeniɛ]
Australia	**Australië**	[ɔustraliɛ]
Austria	**Oostenryk**	[oəstenrajk]
Azerbaijan	**Azerbeidjan**	[azerbæjdjan]
The Bahamas	**die Bahamas**	[di bahamas]
Bangladesh	**Bangladesj**	[bangladeʃ]
Belarus	**Belarus**	[belarus]
Belgium	**België**	[belχiɛ]
Bolivia	**Bolivië**	[boliviɛ]
Bosnia and Herzegovina	**Bosnië & Herzegowina**	[bosniɛ en hersegovina]
Brazil	**Brasilië**	[brasiliɛ]
Bulgaria	**Bulgarye**	[bulχaraje]
Cambodia	**Kambodja**	[kambodja]
Canada	**Kanada**	[kanada]
Chile	**Chili**	[tʃili]
China	**Sjina**	[ʃina]
Colombia	**Colombia, Kolombië**	[kolombia], [kolombiɛ]
Croatia	**Kroasië**	[kroasiɛ]
Cuba	**Kuba**	[kuba]
Cyprus	**Ciprus**	[siprus]
Czech Republic	**Tjeggië**	[tʃeχiɛ]
Denmark	**Denemarke**	[denemarkə]
Dominican Republic	**Dominikaanse Republiek**	[dominikãŋsə republik]
Ecuador	**Ecuador**	[ɛkuador]
Egypt	**Egipte**	[ɛχiptə]
England	**Engeland**	[ɛŋəlant]
Estonia	**Estland**	[ɛstlant]
Finland	**Finland**	[finlant]
France	**Frankryk**	[frankrajk]
French Polynesia	**Frans-Polinesië**	[fraŋs-polinesiɛ]
Georgia	**Georgië**	[χeorχiɛ]
Germany	**Duitsland**	[dœitslant]
Ghana	**Ghana**	[χana]
Great Britain	**Groot-Brittanje**	[χroət-brittanje]
Greece	**Griekeland**	[χrikəlant]
Haiti	**Haïti**	[haïti]
Hungary	**Hongarye**	[honχaraje]

100. Countries. Part 2

Iceland	Ysland	[ajslant]
India	Indië	[indiɛ]
Indonesia	Indonesië	[indonesiɛ]
Iran	Iran	[iran]
Iraq	Irak	[irak]
Ireland	Ierland	[irlant]
Israel	Israel	[israəl]
Italy	Italië	[italiɛ]
Jamaica	Jamaika	[jamajka]
Japan	Japan	[japan]
Jordan	Jordanië	[jordaniɛ]
Kazakhstan	Kazakstan	[kasakstan]
Kenya	Kenia	[kenia]
Kirghizia	Kirgisië	[kirχisiɛ]
Kuwait	Kuwait	[kuvajt]
Laos	Laos	[laos]
Latvia	Letland	[letlant]
Lebanon	Libanon	[libanon]
Libya	Libië	[libiɛ]
Liechtenstein	Lichtenstein	[liχtɛŋstejn]
Lithuania	Litoue	[litæʊə]
Luxembourg	Luksemburg	[luksemburχ]
Macedonia (Republic of ~)	Masedonië	[masedoniɛ]
Madagascar	Madagaskar	[madaχaskar]
Malaysia	Maleisië	[malæjsiɛ]
Malta	Malta	[malta]
Mexico	Meksiko	[meksiko]
Moldova, Moldavia	Moldawië	[moldaviɛ]
Monaco	Monako	[monako]
Mongolia	Mongolië	[monχoliɛ]
Montenegro	Montenegro	[montənegro]
Morocco	Marokko	[marokko]
Myanmar	Myanmar	[mjanmar]
Namibia	Namibië	[namibiɛ]
Nepal	Nepal	[nepal]
Netherlands	Nederland	[nedərlant]
New Zealand	Nieu-Seeland	[niu-seəlant]
North Korea	Noord-Korea	[noərd-korea]
Norway	Noorweë	[noərweɛ]

101. Countries. Part 3

| Pakistan | Pakistan | [pakistan] |
| Palestine | Palestina | [palestina] |

Panama	**Panama**	[panama]
Paraguay	**Paraguay**	[paragwaj]
Peru	**Peru**	[peru]
Poland	**Pole**	[polə]
Portugal	**Portugal**	[portuχal]
Romania	**Roemenië**	[rumeniɛ]
Russia	**Rusland**	[ruslant]
Saudi Arabia	**Saoedi-Arabië**	[saudi-arabiɛ]
Scotland	**Skotland**	[skotlant]
Senegal	**Senegal**	[seneχal]
Serbia	**Serwië**	[serwiɛ]
Slovakia	**Slowakye**	[slovakajə]
Slovenia	**Slovenië**	[slofeniɛ]
South Africa	**Suid-Afrika**	[sœid-afrika]
South Korea	**Suid-Korea**	[sœid-korea]
Spain	**Spanje**	[spanjə]
Suriname	**Suriname**	[surinamə]
Sweden	**Swede**	[swedə]
Switzerland	**Switserland**	[switsərlant]
Syria	**Sirië**	[siriɛ]
Taiwan	**Taiwan**	[tajvan]
Tajikistan	**Tadjikistan**	[tadʒikistan]
Tanzania	**Tanzanië**	[tansaniɛ]
Tasmania	**Tasmanië**	[tasmaniɛ]
Thailand	**Thailand**	[tajlant]
Tunisia	**Tunisië**	[tunisiɛ]
Turkey	**Turkye**	[turkajə]
Turkmenistan	**Turkmenistan**	[turkmenistan]
Ukraine	**Oekraïne**	[ukraïnə]
United Arab Emirates	**Verenigde Arabiese Emirate**	[fereniχdə arabisə emiratə]
United States of America	**Verenigde State van Amerika**	[fereniχdə statə fan amerika]
Uruguay	**Uruguay**	[urugwaj]
Uzbekistan	**Oezbekistan**	[uzbekistan]
Vatican	**Vatikaan**	[fatikãn]
Venezuela	**Venezuela**	[fenesuela]
Vietnam	**Viëtnam**	[viɛtnam]
Zanzibar	**Zanzibar**	[zanzibar]

GASTRONOMIC GLOSSARY

This section contains a lot of
words and terms associated
with food. This dictionary will
make it easier for you to
understand the menu at a
restaurant and choose
the right dish

T&P Books Publishing

English-Afrikaans gastronomic glossary

aftertaste	nasmaak	[nasmāk]
almond	amandel	[amandəl]
anise	anys	[anajs]
aperitif	drankie	[dranki]
appetite	aptyt	[aptajt]
appetizer	voorgereg	[foərχerəχ]
apple	appel	[appəl]
apricot	appelkoos	[appɛlkoəs]
artichoke	artisjok	[artiʃok]
asparagus	aspersie	[aspersi]
Atlantic salmon	atlantiese salm	[atlantisə salm]
avocado	avokado	[afokado]
bacon	spek	[spek]
banana	piesang	[pisaŋ]
barley	gars	[χars]
bartender	kroegman	[kruχman]
basil	basilikum	[basilikum]
bay leaf	lourierblaar	[læʊrir·blār]
beans	boontjies	[boənkis]
beef	beesvleis	[beəs·flæjs]
beer	bier	[bir]
beetroot	beet	[beət]
bell pepper	paprika	[paprika]
berries	bessies	[bɛssis]
berry	bessie	[bɛssi]
bilberry	bosbessie	[bosbɛssi]
birch bolete	berkboleet	[berk·boleət]
bitter	bitter	[bittər]
black coffee	swart koffie	[swart koffi]
black pepper	swart peper	[swart pepər]
black tea	swart tee	[swart teə]
blackberry	braambessie	[brāmbɛssi]
blackcurrant	swartbessie	[swartbɛssi]
boiled	gekook	[χekoək]
bottle opener	botteloopmaker	[bottəl·oəpmakər]
bread	brood	[broət]
breakfast	ontbyt	[ontbajt]
bream	brasem	[brasem]
broccoli	broccoli	[brokoli]
Brussels sprouts	Brusselspruite	[brussɛl·sprœitə]
buckwheat	bokwiet	[bokwit]
butter	botter	[bottər]
buttercream	crème	[krɛm]
cabbage	kool	[koəl]

cake	koek	[kuk]
cake	koek	[kuk]
calorie	kalorie	[kalori]
can opener	blikoopmaker	[blik·oəpmakər]
candy	lekkers	[lɛkkərs]
canned food	blikkieskos	[blikkis·kos]
cappuccino	capuccino	[kaputʃino]
caraway	komynsaad	[komajnsāt]
carbohydrates	koolhidrate	[koəlhidratə]
carbonated	soda-	[soda-]
carp	karp	[karp]
carrot	wortel	[vortəl]
catfish	katvis, seebaber	[katfis], [see·babər]
cauliflower	blomkool	[blom·koəl]
caviar	kaviaar	[kafiār]
celery	seldery	[selderaj]
cep	Eetbare boleet	[eətbarə boleət]
cereal crops	graangewasse	[χrān·χəwassə]
cereal grains	ontbytgraan	[ontbajt·χrān]
champagne	sjampanje	[ʃampanje]
chanterelle	dooierswam	[dojer·swam]
check	rekening	[rekəniŋ]
cheese	kaas	[kās]
chewing gum	kougom	[kæʋχom]
chicken	hoender	[hundər]
chocolate	sjokolade	[ʃokoladə]
chocolate	sjokolade	[ʃokoladə]
cinnamon	kaneel	[kaneəl]
clear soup	helder sop	[hɛldər sop]
cloves	naeltjies	[naɛlkis]
cocktail	mengeldrankie	[menχəl·dranki]
coconut	klapper	[klappər]
cod	kabeljou	[kabeljæʋ]
coffee	koffie	[koffi]
coffee with milk	koffie met melk	[koffi met melk]
cognac	brandewyn	[brandə·vajn]
cold	koud	[kæʋt]
condensed milk	kondensmelk	[kondɛŋs·melk]
condiment	smaakmiddel	[smāk·middəl]
confectionery	soet gebak	[sut χebak]
cookies	koekies	[kukis]
coriander	koljander	[koljandər]
corkscrew	kurktrekker	[kurk·trɛkkər]
corn	mielie	[mili]
corn	mielie	[mili]
cornflakes	mielievlokkies	[mili·flokkis]
course, dish	gereg	[χerəχ]
cowberry	pryselbessie	[prajsɛlbɛssi]
crab	krab	[krap]
cranberry	bosbessie	[bosbɛssi]
cream	room	[roəm]
crumb	krummel	[krumməl]

crustaceans	skaaldiere	[skāldirə]
cucumber	komkommer	[komkommər]
cuisine	kookkuns	[koək·kuns]
cup	koppie	[koppi]
dark beer	donker bier	[donkər bir]
date	dadel	[dadəl]
death cap	duiwelsbrood	[dœivɛls·broət]
dessert	nagereg	[naχerəχ]
diet	dieet	[diət]
dill	dille	[dillə]
dinner	aandete	[āndetə]
dried	gedroog	[χedroəχ]
drinking water	drinkwater	[drink·vatər]
duck	eend	[eent]
ear	aar	[ār]
edible mushroom	eetbare paddastoel	[eətbarə paddastul]
eel	paling	[paliŋ]
egg	eier	[æjer]
egg white	eierwit	[æjer·wit]
egg yolk	dooier	[dojer]
eggplant	eiervrug	[æjerfruχ]
eggs	eiers	[æjers]
Enjoy your meal!	Smaaklike ete!	[smāklikə etə!]
fats	vette	[fɛttə]
fig	vy	[faj]
filling	vulsel	[fulsəl]
fish	vis	[fis]
flatfish	platvis	[platfis]
flour	meelblom	[meəl·blom]
fly agaric	vlieëswam	[fliɛ·swam]
food	kos	[kos]
fork	vurk	[furk]
freshly squeezed juice	vars geparste sap	[fars χeparstə sap]
fried	gebak	[χebak]
fried eggs	gabakte eiers	[χabaktə æjers]
frozen	gevries	[χefris]
fruit	vrugte	[fruχtə]
fruits	vrugte	[fruχtə]
game	wild	[vilt]
gammon	gerookte ham	[χeroəktə ham]
garlic	knoffel	[knoffəl]
gin	jenever	[jenefər]
ginger	gemmer	[χɛmmər]
glass	glas	[χlas]
glass	wynglas	[vajn·χlas]
goose	gans	[χaŋs]
gooseberry	appelliefie	[appɛllifi]
grain	graan	[χrān]
grape	druif	[drœif]
grapefruit	pomelo	[pomelo]
green tea	groen tee	[χrun teə]
greens	groente	[χruntə]

halibut	heilbot	[hæjlbot]
ham	ham	[ham]
hamburger	maalvleis	[māl·flæjs]
hamburger	hamburger	[hamburχər]
hazelnut	haselneut	[hasɛl·nøət]
herring	haring	[hariŋ]
honey	heuning	[høəniŋ]
horseradish	peperwortel	[peper·wortəl]
hot	warm	[varm]
ice	ys	[ajs]
ice-cream	roomys	[roəm·ajs]
instant coffee	poeierkoffie	[pujer·koffi]
jam	konfyt	[konfajt]
jam	konfyt	[konfajt]
juice	sap	[sap]
kidney bean	nierboontjie	[nir·boənki]
kiwi	kiwi, kiwivrug	[kivi], [kivi·fruχ]
knife	mes	[mes]
lamb	lamsvleis	[lams·flæjs]
lemon	suurlemoen	[sɪr·lemun]
lemonade	limonade	[limonadə]
lentil	lensie	[lɛŋsi]
lettuce	slaai	[slāi]
light beer	ligte bier	[liχtə bir]
liqueur	likeur	[likøər]
liquors	likeure	[likøərə]
liver	lewer	[levər]
lunch	middagete	[middaχ·etə]
mackerel	makriel	[makril]
mandarin	nartjie	[narki]
mango	mango	[manχo]
margarine	margarien	[marχarin]
marmalade	marmelade	[marmeladə]
mashed potatoes	kapokaartappels	[kapok·ārtappəls]
mayonnaise	mayonnaise	[majonɛs]
meat	vleis	[flæjs]
melon	spanspek	[spaŋspek]
menu	spyskaart	[spajs·kārt]
milk	melk	[melk]
milkshake	melkskommel	[melk·skomməl]
millet	gierst	[χirst]
mineral water	mineraalwater	[minerāl·vatər]
morel	morielje	[morilje]
mushroom	paddastoel	[paddastul]
mustard	mosterd	[mostert]
non-alcoholic	nie-alkoholies	[ni-alkoholis]
noodles	noedels	[nudɛls]
oats	hawer	[havər]
olive oil	olyfolie	[olajf·oli]
olives	olywe	[olajvə]
omelet	omelet	[oməlet]
onion	ui	[œi]

orange	lemoen	[lemun]
orange juice	lemoensap	[lemoən·sap]
orange-cap boletus	rooihoed	[rojhut]
oyster	oester	[ustər]
pâté	patee	[pateə]
papaya	papaja	[papaja]
paprika	paprika	[paprika]
parsley	pietersielie	[pitərsili]
pasta	pasta	[pasta]
pea	ertjie	[ɛrki]
peach	perske	[perskə]
peanut	grondboontjie	[xront·boənki]
pear	peer	[peər]
peel	skil	[skil]
perch	baars	[bārs]
pickled	gepiekel	[xepikəl]
pie	pastei	[pastæj]
piece	stuk	[stuk]
pike	varswatersnoek	[farswatər·snuk]
pike perch	varswatersnoek	[farswatər·snuk]
pineapple	pynappel	[pajnappəl]
pistachios	pistachio	[pistatʃio]
pizza	pizza	[pizza]
plate	bord	[bort]
plum	pruim	[prœim]
poisonous mushroom	giftige paddastoel	[xiftiχə paddastul]
pomegranate	granaat	[xranāt]
pork	varkvleis	[fark·flæjs]
porridge	pap	[pap]
portion	porsie	[porsi]
potato	aartappel	[ārtappəl]
proteins	proteïen	[proteïen]
pub, bar	kroeg	[kruχ]
pudding	poeding	[pudiŋ]
pumpkin	pampoen	[pampun]
rabbit	konynvleis	[konajn·flæjs]
radish	radys	[radajs]
raisin	rosyntjie	[rosajnki]
raspberry	framboos	[framboəs]
recipe	resep	[resep]
red pepper	rooi peper	[roj pepər]
red wine	rooiwyn	[roj·vajn]
redcurrant	rooi aalbessie	[roj ālbɛssi]
refreshing drink	verfrissende drank	[ferfrissendə drank]
rice	rys	[rajs]
rum	rum	[rum]
russula	russula	[russula]
rye	rog	[roχ]
saffron	saffraan	[saffrān]
salad	slaai	[slāi]
salmon	salm	[salm]
salt	sout	[sæʋt]

salty	**sout**	[sæʊt]
sandwich	**toebroodjie**	[tubroədʒi]
sardine	**sardyn**	[sardajn]
sauce	**sous**	[sæʊs]
saucer	**piering**	[piriŋ]
sausage	**wors**	[vors]
seafood	**seekos**	[seə·kos]
sesame	**sesamsaad**	[sesam·sāt]
shark	**haai**	[hāi]
shrimp	**garnaal**	[χarnāl]
side dish	**sygereg**	[saj·χerəχ]
slice	**snytjie**	[snajki]
smoked	**gerook**	[χeroək]
soft drink	**koeldrank**	[kul·drank]
soup	**sop**	[sop]
soup spoon	**soplepel**	[sop·lepəl]
sour cherry	**suurkersie**	[sɪr·kersi]
sour cream	**suurroom**	[sɪr·roəm]
soy	**soja**	[soja]
spaghetti	**spaghetti**	[spaχɛtti]
sparkling	**bruis-**	[brœis-]
spice	**spesery**	[spesəraj]
spinach	**spinasie**	[spinasi]
spiny lobster	**seekreef**	[seə·kreəf]
spoon	**lepel**	[lepəl]
squid	**pylinkvis**	[pajl·inkfis]
steak	**biefstuk**	[bifstuk]
still	**sonder gas**	[sondər χas]
strawberry	**aarbei**	[ārbæj]
sturgeon	**steur**	[støər]
sugar	**suiker**	[sœikər]
sunflower oil	**sonblomolie**	[sonblom·oli]
sweet	**soet**	[sut]
sweet cherry	**soetkersie**	[sut·kersi]
taste, flavor	**smaak**	[smāk]
tasty	**smaaklik**	[smāklik]
tea	**tee**	[teə]
teaspoon	**teelepeltjie**	[teə·lepəlki]
tip	**fooitjie**	[fojki]
tomato	**tamatie**	[tamati]
tomato juice	**tamatiesap**	[tamati·sap]
tongue	**tong**	[toŋ]
toothpick	**tandestokkie**	[tandə·stokki]
trout	**forel**	[forəl]
tuna	**tuna**	[tuna]
turkey	**kalkoen**	[kalkun]
turnip	**raap**	[rāp]
veal	**kalfsvleis**	[kalfs·flæjs]
vegetable oil	**plantaardige olie**	[plantārdiχə oli]
vegetables	**groente**	[χruntə]
vegetarian	**vegetariër**	[feχetariɛr]
vegetarian	**vegetaries**	[feχetaris]

vermouth	vermoet	[fermut]
vienna sausage	Weense worsie	[veɛŋsə vorsi]
vinegar	asyn	[asajn]
vitamin	vitamien	[fitamin]
vodka	vodka	[fodka]
waffles	wafels	[vafɛls]
waiter	kelner	[kɛlnər]
waitress	kelnerin	[kɛlnərin]
walnut	okkerneut	[okkər·nøət]
water	water	[vatər]
watermelon	waatlemoen	[vātlemun]
wheat	koring	[koriŋ]
whiskey	whisky	[vhiskaj]
white wine	witwyn	[vit·vajn]
wild strawberry	wilde aarbei	[vildə ārbæj]
wine	wyn	[vajn]
wine list	wyn	[vajn]
with ice	met ys	[mɛt ajs]
yogurt	jogurt	[joχurt]
zucchini	vingerskorsie	[fiŋər·skorsi]

Afrikaans-English gastronomic glossary

aandete	[āndetə]	dinner
aar	[ār]	ear
aarbei	[ārbæj]	strawberry
aartappel	[ārtappəl]	potato
amandel	[amandəl]	almond
anys	[anajs]	anise
appel	[appəl]	apple
appelkoos	[appɛlkoəs]	apricot
appelliefie	[appɛllifi]	gooseberry
aptyt	[aptajt]	appetite
artisjok	[artiʃok]	artichoke
aspersie	[aspersi]	asparagus
asyn	[asajn]	vinegar
atlantiese salm	[atlantisə salm]	Atlantic salmon
avokado	[afokado]	avocado
baars	[bārs]	perch
basilikum	[basilikum]	basil
beesvleis	[beəs·flæjs]	beef
beet	[beət]	beetroot
berkboleet	[berk·boleət]	birch bolete
bessie	[bɛssi]	berry
bessies	[bɛssis]	berries
biefstuk	[bifstuk]	steak
bier	[bir]	beer
bitter	[bittər]	bitter
blikkieskos	[blikkis·kos]	canned food
blikoopmaker	[blik·oəpmakər]	can opener
blomkool	[blom·koəl]	cauliflower
bokwiet	[bokwit]	buckwheat
boontjies	[boənkis]	beans
bord	[bort]	plate
bosbessie	[bosbɛssi]	bilberry
bosbessie	[bosbɛssi]	cranberry
botteloopmaker	[bottel·oəpmakər]	bottle opener
botter	[bottər]	butter
braambessie	[brāmbɛssi]	blackberry
brandewyn	[brandə·vajn]	cognac
brasem	[brasem]	bream
broccoli	[brokoli]	broccoli
brood	[broət]	bread
bruis-	[brœis-]	sparkling
Brusselspruite	[brussɛl·sprœitə]	Brussels sprouts
capuccino	[kaputʃino]	cappuccino
crème	[krɛm]	buttercream

dadel	[dadəl]	date
dieet	[diət]	diet
dille	[dillə]	dill
donker bier	[donkər bir]	dark beer
dooier	[dojer]	egg yolk
dooierswam	[dojer·swam]	chanterelle
drankie	[dranki]	aperitif
drinkwater	[drink·vatər]	drinking water
druif	[drœif]	grape
duiwelsbrood	[dœivɛls·broət]	death cap
eend	[eent]	duck
Eetbare boleet	[eətbarə boleət]	cep
eetbare paddastoel	[eətbarə paddastul]	edible mushroom
eier	[æjer]	egg
eiers	[æjers]	eggs
eiervrug	[æjerfruχ]	eggplant
eierwit	[æjer·wit]	egg white
ertjie	[ɛrki]	pea
fooitjie	[fojki]	tip
forel	[forəl]	trout
framboos	[framboəs]	raspberry
gabakte eiers	[χabaktə æjers]	fried eggs
gans	[χaŋs]	goose
garnaal	[χarnāl]	shrimp
gars	[χars]	barley
gebak	[χebak]	fried
gedroog	[χedroəχ]	dried
gekook	[χekoək]	boiled
gemmer	[χɛmmər]	ginger
gepiekel	[χepikəl]	pickled
gereg	[χerəχ]	course, dish
gerook	[χeroək]	smoked
gerookte ham	[χeroəktə ham]	gammon
gevries	[χefris]	frozen
gierst	[χirst]	millet
giftige paddastoel	[χiftiχə paddastul]	poisonous mushroom
glas	[χlas]	glass
graan	[χrān]	grain
graangewasse	[χrān·χəwassə]	cereal crops
granaat	[χranāt]	pomegranate
groen tee	[χrun teə]	green tea
groente	[χruntə]	vegetables
groente	[χruntə]	greens
grondboontjie	[χront·boənki]	peanut
haai	[hāi]	shark
ham	[ham]	ham
hamburger	[hamburχər]	hamburger
haring	[hariŋ]	herring
haselneut	[hasɛl·nøət]	hazelnut
hawer	[havər]	oats
heilbot	[hæjlbot]	halibut
helder sop	[hɛldər sop]	clear soup

heuning	[høənin]	honey
hoender	[hundər]	chicken
jenever	[jenefər]	gin
jogurt	[joɣurt]	yogurt
kaas	[kãs]	cheese
kabeljou	[kabeljæʊ]	cod
kalfsvleis	[kalfs·flæjs]	veal
kalkoen	[kalkun]	turkey
kalorie	[kalori]	calorie
kaneel	[kaneəl]	cinnamon
kapokaartappels	[kapok·ãrtappəls]	mashed potatoes
karp	[karp]	carp
katvis, seebaber	[katfis], [seə·babər]	catfish
kaviaar	[kafiãr]	caviar
kelner	[kɛlnər]	waiter
kelnerin	[kɛlnərin]	waitress
kiwi, kiwivrug	[kivi], [kivi·fruɣ]	kiwi
klapper	[klappər]	coconut
knoffel	[knoffəl]	garlic
koek	[kuk]	cake
koek	[kuk]	cake
koekies	[kukis]	cookies
koeldrank	[kul·drank]	soft drink
koffie	[koffi]	coffee
koffie met melk	[koffi met melk]	coffee with milk
koljander	[koljandər]	coriander
komkommer	[komkommər]	cucumber
komynsaad	[komajnsãt]	caraway
kondensmelk	[kondɛŋs·melk]	condensed milk
konfyt	[konfajt]	jam
konfyt	[konfajt]	jam
konynvleis	[konajn·flæjs]	rabbit
kookkuns	[koək·kuns]	cuisine
kool	[koəl]	cabbage
koolhidrate	[koəlhidratə]	carbohydrates
koppie	[koppi]	cup
koring	[korin]	wheat
kos	[kos]	food
koud	[kæʊt]	cold
kougom	[kæʊɣom]	chewing gum
krab	[krap]	crab
kroeg	[kruɣ]	pub, bar
kroegman	[kruɣman]	bartender
krummel	[krumməl]	crumb
kurktrekker	[kurk·trɛkkər]	corkscrew
lamsvleis	[lams·flæjs]	lamb
lekkers	[lɛkkərs]	candy
lemoen	[lemun]	orange
lemoensap	[lemoən·sap]	orange juice
lensie	[lɛŋsi]	lentil
lepel	[lepəl]	spoon
lewer	[levər]	liver

ligte bier	[liҳtə bir]	light beer
likeur	[likøər]	liqueur
likeure	[likøərə]	liquors
limonade	[limonadə]	lemonade
lourierblaar	[læurir·blār]	bay leaf
maalvleis	[māl·flæjs]	hamburger
makriel	[makril]	mackerel
mango	[manҳo]	mango
margarien	[marҳarin]	margarine
marmelade	[marmeladə]	marmalade
mayonnaise	[majonɛs]	mayonnaise
meelblom	[meəl·blom]	flour
melk	[mɛlk]	milk
melkskommel	[mɛlk·skomməl]	milkshake
mengeldrankie	[menҳəl·dranki]	cocktail
mes	[mes]	knife
met ys	[met ajs]	with ice
middagete	[middaҳ·etə]	lunch
mielie	[mili]	corn
mielie	[mili]	corn
mielievlokkies	[mili·flokkis]	cornflakes
mineraalwater	[minerāl·vatər]	mineral water
morielje	[morilje]	morel
mosterd	[mostert]	mustard
naeltjies	[naɛlkis]	cloves
nagereg	[naҳerəҳ]	dessert
nartjie	[narki]	mandarin
nasmaak	[nasmāk]	aftertaste
nie-alkoholies	[ni-alkoholis]	non-alcoholic
nierboontjie	[nir·boənki]	kidney bean
noedels	[nudɛls]	noodles
oester	[ustər]	oyster
okkerneut	[okkər·nøət]	walnut
olyfolie	[olajf·oli]	olive oil
olywe	[olajvə]	olives
omelet	[oməlet]	omelet
ontbyt	[ontbajt]	breakfast
ontbytgraan	[ontbajt·ҳrān]	cereal grains
paddastoel	[paddastul]	mushroom
paling	[paliŋ]	eel
pampoen	[pampun]	pumpkin
pap	[pap]	porridge
papaja	[papaja]	papaya
paprika	[paprika]	bell pepper
paprika	[paprika]	paprika
pasta	[pasta]	pasta
pastei	[pastæj]	pie
patee	[pateə]	pâté
peer	[peər]	pear
peperwortel	[peper·wortəl]	horseradish
perske	[perskə]	peach
piering	[piriŋ]	saucer

piesang	[pisaŋ]	banana
pietersielie	[pitərsili]	parsley
pistachio	[pistatʃio]	pistachios
pizza	[pizza]	pizza
plantaardige olie	[plantārdiχə oli]	vegetable oil
platvis	[platfis]	flatfish
poeding	[pudiŋ]	pudding
poeierkoffie	[pujer·koffi]	instant coffee
pomelo	[pomelo]	grapefruit
porsie	[porsi]	portion
proteïen	[proteïen]	proteins
pruim	[prœim]	plum
pryselbessie	[prajsɛlbɛssi]	cowberry
pylinkvis	[pajl·inkfis]	squid
pynappel	[pajnappəl]	pineapple
raap	[rāp]	turnip
radys	[radajs]	radish
rekening	[rekəniŋ]	check
resep	[resep]	recipe
rog	[roχ]	rye
rooi aalbessie	[roj ālbɛssi]	redcurrant
rooi peper	[roj pepər]	red pepper
rooihoed	[rojhut]	orange-cap boletus
rooiwyn	[roj·vajn]	red wine
room	[roəm]	cream
roomys	[roəm·ajs]	ice-cream
rosyntjie	[rosajnki]	raisin
rum	[rum]	rum
russula	[russula]	russula
rys	[rajs]	rice
saffraan	[saffrān]	saffron
salm	[salm]	salmon
sap	[sap]	juice
sardyn	[sardajn]	sardine
seekos	[seə·kos]	seafood
seekreef	[seə·kreəf]	spiny lobster
seldery	[selderaj]	celery
sesamsaad	[sesam·sāt]	sesame
sjampanje	[ʃampanje]	champagne
sjokolade	[ʃokoladə]	chocolate
sjokolade	[ʃokoladə]	chocolate
skaaldiere	[skāldirə]	crustaceans
skil	[skil]	peel
slaai	[slāi]	lettuce
slaai	[slāi]	salad
smaak	[smāk]	taste, flavor
smaaklik	[smāklik]	tasty
Smaaklike ete!	[smāklikə etə!]	Enjoy your meal!
smaakmiddel	[smāk·middəl]	condiment
snytjie	[snajki]	slice
soda-	[soda-]	carbonated
soet	[sut]	sweet

soet gebak	[sut χebak]	confectionery
soetkersie	[sut·kersi]	sweet cherry
soja	[soja]	soy
sonblomolie	[sonblom·oli]	sunflower oil
sonder gas	[sondər χas]	still
sop	[sop]	soup
soplepel	[sop·lepəl]	soup spoon
sous	[sæʊs]	sauce
sout	[sæʊt]	salt
sout	[sæʊt]	salty
spaghetti	[spaχɛtti]	spaghetti
spanspek	[spaŋspek]	melon
spek	[spek]	bacon
spesery	[spesəraj]	spice
spinasie	[spinasi]	spinach
spyskaart	[spajs·kārt]	menu
steur	[støər]	sturgeon
stuk	[stuk]	piece
suiker	[sœikər]	sugar
suurkersie	[sɪr·kersi]	sour cherry
suurlemoen	[sɪr·lemun]	lemon
suurroom	[sɪr·roəm]	sour cream
swart koffie	[swart koffi]	black coffee
swart peper	[swart pepər]	black pepper
swart tee	[swart teə]	black tea
swartbessie	[swartbɛssi]	blackcurrant
sygereg	[saj·χerəχ]	side dish
tamatie	[tamati]	tomato
tamatiesap	[tamati·sap]	tomato juice
tandestokkie	[tandə·stokki]	toothpick
tee	[teə]	tea
teelepeltjie	[teə·lepəlki]	teaspoon
toebroodjie	[tubroədʒi]	sandwich
tong	[toŋ]	tongue
tuna	[tuna]	tuna
ui	[œi]	onion
varkvleis	[fark·flæjs]	pork
vars geparste sap	[fars χeparstə sap]	freshly squeezed juice
varswatersnoek	[farswatər·snuk]	pike
varswatersnoek	[farswatər·snuk]	pike perch
vegetariër	[feχetariɛr]	vegetarian
vegetaries	[feχetaris]	vegetarian
verfrissende drank	[ferfrissendə drank]	refreshing drink
vermoet	[fermut]	vermouth
vette	[fɛttə]	fats
vingerskorsie	[fiŋər·skorsi]	zucchini
vis	[fis]	fish
vitamien	[fitamin]	vitamin
vleis	[flæjs]	meat
vlieëswam	[fliɛ·swam]	fly agaric
vodka	[fodka]	vodka
voorgereg	[foərχerəχ]	appetizer

vrugte	[fruχtə]	fruit
vrugte	[fruχtə]	fruits
vulsel	[fulsəl]	filling
vurk	[furk]	fork
vy	[faj]	fig
waatlemoen	[vātlemun]	watermelon
wafels	[vafɛls]	waffles
warm	[varm]	hot
water	[vatər]	water
Weense worsie	[veɛŋsə vorsi]	vienna sausage
whisky	[vhiskaj]	whiskey
wild	[vilt]	game
wilde aarbei	[vildə ārbæj]	wild strawberry
witwyn	[vit·vajn]	white wine
wors	[vors]	sausage
wortel	[vortəl]	carrot
wyn	[vajn]	wine
wyn	[vajn]	wine list
wynglas	[vajn·χlas]	glass
ys	[ajs]	ice

37254767R00114

Printed in Great Britain
by Amazon